Secure at Last

Overcoming Life's Tragedies

by Sherry Francis

Double Portion Publishing

Secure at Last

by Sherry Francis

ISBN 9798391366522

Copyright 2022, 2023 by Sherry Francis

Contents

Thanksgiving Plans Gone Wrong 1

Calm Years Before the Storm 9

The End of Pollyanna................................. 17

Little Girls Grow Up to Be Big Girls........... 25

Crumbling Walls 33

A Radical Complete Healing 45

Teacher: Ms Hall....................................... 55

Marriage and Family 101 59

Made in Singapore 68

Mama Love 77

Black Friday... 83

Bula Vinaka! Fiji, Here We Come! 95

Culture and Ministry 109

Scary Times.. 125

Crossroads 131

Melissa's Fight for Health.......................... 143

Love and Betrayal 149

Walking Toward Healing............................ 167

My Life Is Amazing................................... 177

Big Challenges Can Lead........................... 186

Acknowledgments

I want to thank my Aunt Bev Caruso. This book never would have happened without her. From her first suggestion that I write a book to her encouraging me to keep going through the long tedious hours, to the proofreading, editing, and publishing. She spent countless hours in every stage of this book without one complaint. Auntie, this book is as much yours as it is mine. Thank you from the bottom of my heart!

A very special thanks to my amazing friend Cindy Kanemoto. With her background in editing and keen writing skills, she provided input into the structure of the book that made it a much better read. Thank you, Cindy, for your wisdom and friendship.

To my cousin Debbie's son, Daniel Peterson. Thank you for the beautiful cover you designed. It makes this a three-generation book. I love it.

To my awesome hubby, Jay Francis. Thank you for taking care of many of my wifely duties so I could spend the countless hours needed to write this book. Your unconditional love and support mean the world to me. I love you with all that I am!

To my two most precious treasures, Nathan Peavy and Melissa Cole. Thank you for your constant love, friendship, and hilarious humor that keeps me laughing. And for those precious grandbabies you have brought into my life—there is no love like it! Mel, thank you for allowing me to use your blog as one of the springboards for this book. I'm so proud of the great adults you two have become!

To my family by marriage: Travis Cole, Melissa Peavy, Katie and Luke Brownell. I couldn't have handpicked more awesome people to marry into our family. Thank you for adding so much joy to our clan.

To my dad, Don Hall. Thank you for showing me by example the Father heart of God: for forgiving me when I felt unforgivable. The outcome of this book would not be the same were it not for you.

To my mom, Patti Hall. Thank you, Ma, for the countless ways you spoke into my life unending love and encouragement. And for teaching me through example that loving others unconditionally is the most important thing we can do in this life. I wouldn't be who I am today without you. I love you. "You are lucky." :))

To my brothers Rick and Steve Hall. Rick, I value our many late-night deep conversations about our lives, our loves, our heartbreaks, and God's will in it all. Steve, thank you for showing me by example how to be an overcomer when life deals you lemons. The smile on your face says it all.

And last but not least, thank you to my cherished friends who have laughed and cried with me through living the life of the pages of this book. Marta Walther, Cheryl Kildebeck, Joy and John Stephan, my "Onya Sisters" (Julie Chafin, Brenda Smith, Shannon Gibbons), cousin/sister Julie Krake, Chris Croll, Connie Mesich, Joni Sleeper, Lynn Alberts, and my extended family. If your name isn't mentioned, please know it is because of the confines of space.

Foreword

Sherry Francis was the effervescent gal, a life of the party at our huge family's holiday gatherings. Oh, I knew of her chronic pain from a car accident several years back, of marital struggles, of the pressures of being the daughter of a public figure, and normal struggles of being a missionary in foreign lands. One would never have guessed that the beautiful blonde who at age sixty was still climbing mountains, riding zip lines, and white-water rafting, had lived through not just one tragedy, but a series of them.

Sherry has always been a vibrant bundle of energy. She loves to tell stories, to both play—and to teach—the piano, and to have fun with family and friends. I am Sherry's aunt, the sister of her dad. Yet I had no idea the depth of heartache she had experienced. She hid things well.

Like me, Sherry married a preacher and ministered in other countries. Yet the depth of sorrows she reveals in this book have surprised me. Sherry is a survivor. In *Secure at Last*, she has laid it all out for everyone to see. For Sherry has learned to completely turn her tragedies over to God. And she has entered into a peace and joy she had never known.

My own kids, grands, and greats were gathered in Texas in 2020, to celebrate Thanksgiving the following day when I received a frantic call from California, from Sherry's mom. Sherry had been in a terrible car accident; she may not survive. We stopped everything and joined in prayer with other extended-family households across the country and even on the other side of the world. We knew prayer was our only hope, but also a very sure hope. We all knew the God who still works wonders.

In this book you'll get to know the little girl who calls her early years a Pollyanna childhood, who married her prince charming and traveled the world, who went from sorrow to sorrow, nearly lost her life, became wheelchair bound – perhaps for life – and today is a radiant example of what it means to be a victor. This book is

Sherry's gift to those who have suffered deep anguish, endured calamity, or known treachery.

As I followed Sherry's physical battles following that horrible car accident, through posts and phone calls, I sensed a book was being lived. As an author myself, and a trainer of writers, I knew Sherry's journey could help others. I emailed her: "Sherry, if you ever want to write a book, let's talk."

Her answer was immediate, "I never wanted to write a book, but if what I've learned can help others...."

You will be stunned by her afflictions, shaken by her anguish, amazed by her tenacity, and warmed by her transparency. Sherry doesn't just tell her story. She takes you with her as she faces racial hatred, sexual violence, and betrayal. She exposes flawed thought patterns that allow turmoil and anguish to linger—and torment. She takes you by the hand along her perilous journey as she gains insight for applying biblical principles, as her view of her tragedies change along with her understanding of God's never-ending love and healing power.

Many who suffer deep sorrow never fully reach inner healing and wholeness. Sherry's journey to peace with God and herself is something you can experience. You too can overcome life's tragedies and be *Secure at Last*.

Beverly Caruso
Sanger, Texas
2023

Chapter 1
November 25, 2020

Thanksgiving Plans Gone Wrong

Opening my swollen eyes, I am startled to see a man standing inches from my face. I can see he is sewing something…no, not just something, he's sewing my face! I flinch back, and he steadies me with a kind voice. "It's going to be ok," he says. "I'm a plastic surgeon and I'm going to blend this stitching into your chin, so the scar doesn't look so bad."

Being pumped full of pain meds, I answer faintly, "Ok," even though I don't have a clue what he is talking about. My eyes try to adjust to the bright light. There are people with white jackets hovering all around me, medical equipment, and tubes everywhere. Closing my eyes, the voices fade, and I am out again.

I wake up the next day with a man standing next to the bed. He is asking if I want a spinal block for my surgeries. "What's a spinal block?" I slur.

"It will numb your legs; so you won't feel any pain."

"Oh yeah, I definitely want some of that," I quickly respond. I ask what the surgeries are for, and his patient, calm voice explains that I was in a car accident, and they were about to take me into the operating room to repair my broken and crushed bones. He asks me if I remember the accident.

I feel like a complete fool when I answer, "Um, no I actually don't. Can you tell me what happened?"

"Well ma'am you were in a bad car accident. You have broken several bones. You have a compound fractured femur, broken tibia, crushed pelvis, broken nose, and broken ribs." My heart starts to beat faster and I'm having a hard time believing that he's talking about ME!

He continues on in a very matter-of-fact voice, "Well, besides what I mentioned, your pelvis is crushed in four places, which is probably the worst part of your injuries, you broke your nose, tore some muscles, and the bottom of your face was laid open. Your gums were separated from your teeth, so the plastic surgeon sewed them back in your mouth. Right now, you are bleeding in your brain, so we really want to keep an eye on that." I blink back tears as the gravity of the situation begins to sink in.

I'm in and out of sleep for the rest of the day, and for some reason don't feel the need to ask any more questions. ICU is a wonderful place. A place where helpful men and women respond instantly to even the flinch of a muscle. Someone is there with you 24/7 to fulfill your every need.

The next evening, they tell me that I will be moving upstairs to a regular hospital room. Again, I feel no need to ask questions as I doze in and out of consciousness. "1, 2, 3 lift!" I hear as they hoist me onto a different bed.

"Owe!!!" I let out a howl. Oh, the pain! *Please don't move me*, I plead in my head. The reality of what has happened slowly begins to seep in. What on earth has happened to me and why can't I move without excruciating pain? It feels as though someone has taken my body and shaken it; like you do when you get your wrinkled clothes out of the dryer. All my body feels disjointed and riddled with pain.

"Hi, I'm Jean, and I'm the nurse on duty today." Nurse Jean seems to be a kind and caring woman. She proceeds to take my vitals. Studying her face, I surmise that all must be good since she doesn't look overly concerned with the results. She proceeds to show me how to work the controls for the bed and says that if I have to go to the bathroom, I should ring the nurse button and she'll come help me. It suddenly dawns on me that I haven't seen my husband Jay since I've been in the hospital.

My car – how did I survive?

"When will I get to see my husband?" I ask expectantly. Her answer sends my heart plummeting.

"I'm sorry, ma'am, but visitors aren't allowed because of the Covid 19 virus. We're in a lockdown."
"But he's not just a visitor; he's my husband," I quietly plead.

"I'm sorry but nobody is allowed in; even family," she responds without even a hint of compassion in her voice. I'm sure she has to deliver that sad news many times each day.

Doesn't she understand how scared and alone I feel? I mean, what if I have to face some horrible news? Doesn't the hospital care that my husband will be worried sick if he can't see how I am doing? I crumble inside with the scared realization that I'm going to remain utterly alone while I'm here.

"I'll be right back to check on you. If you need anything, just ring the button and I will come back."

Feeling grateful that my nurse is right around the corner helps, and I relax a bit. Lying back in the bed I try very hard to remember the accident. But the only thing that surfaces is a flash picture of me and Chloe leaning to the left side of the car. Chloe is my 15-year-old constant companion dog. She had been with me through a very dark time a few years earlier when my former husband had suddenly died. (More about that later.) At this moment, the only recollection of the accident I have is this picture of Chloe and me. That's all I can call to memory of the last two days.

Just then I hear the phone ring. I note that it's strange to be answering an actual handheld phone. The voice on the other end sends me into tears. It's my husband Jay! We both cry for a bit together. Through tears he squeaks out "Honey I'm so glad you're alive. I was so scared. How are you feeling?"

"I'm doing ok, Babe," I say with as much strength and conviction as I can muster.

"Honey, it is so good to hear your voice! I have no idea what happened since I was at work when the hospital called. Where were you going?"

I fill him in with as much detail as I can remember. I tell him that I was on my way to take a table and some extra chairs to my daughter Mel's house, only 20 minutes away, for our Thanksgiving celebration the next day. We cry a little more and tell each other our *I-love-yous,* before we hang up. My tolerance for interaction and noise is very short and all I want to do now is sleep.

The next day when Jay calls, he fills me in on what the police have told him about the accident. He says that I had made a hard left into oncoming traffic and had been t-boned by an oncoming Volvo SUV. The impact of both vehicles going 50 mph had ejected me through the sunroof and landed me into a field of barbed wired fence. Apparently, I wasn't wearing my seatbelt. (More about that later.)

For the next couple of days, my only interaction with another person besides the nurses was my roommate Dawn, who slept on the other side of a curtain. Strange how fast you bond with a person when you are both groaning in pain together and not sure of your outcome. We talked sporadically about our lives. Mostly about the pain we were each having and why we were there. I found out that her kidneys were failing, and she was going to have a long road ahead of her. As for me, I had no idea what was ahead for me.

For potty issues, we each had a commode next to our bed. On the fourth day, the nurse asked if I wanted her to wheel me into the bathroom. That sounded much better than a bed commode, so I took her up on it. On the way there, my roommate Dawn and I saw each other for the first time. "Oh, so that's what you look like," I laughingly teased.

She cocked her head sideways and said rather slowly, "Uh, you might want to take a look at yourself in the mirror when you go to the bathroom." I waved her off and flippantly replied "I don't really care to do that now. I have enough trouble to worry about."

"Ok, suit yourself, but I really think you should, because a nurse needs to clean you up."

On the second trip to the bathroom, I decided to take a peek. "Holy crap," I screamed. "No wonder you were concerned about my face." It was like I was looking at somebody else. My face had been in a battle with the road, and the road had won. The strange thing is, I really didn't care. And for a woman who always took care of herself and cared about how she looked, this was quite a change.

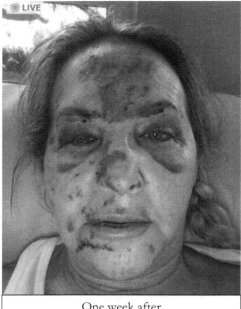
One week after

I thought back to what the plastic surgeon had told me when he was sewing up my face. "Hold still honey. I'm trying to put your face back together. Your lip and chin have been cut away from your face leaving your gums on the outside. If I put everything back together right, I'm hoping the scar will just look like you have another chin." He proceeded to double-stitch my gums back into the inside of my mouth and stitch my lip and chin back together on the outside. I couldn't feel anything from the chin up to my nose. It was just one big swollen blob of stitched up fleshy mess.

My eyes were swollen almost shut with big black circles underneath resulting from the broken nose. The rest of my face was covered in road rash and glass cuts. Now I realized why it was so hard to pronounce words. Dawn told me matter-of-factly that she was going to call the nurse and have her come clean me up, so I complacently complied. Nurse Jean came back in and wheeled me to the sink. She carefully leaned my head back until my hair was in the water and gently tried to rub away the blood that stuck to my hair. Some areas were so matted with blood that she simply had to cut the hair out.

A few days later I learned that I needed to give myself a shot every day for a month. I convinced the doctors that I simply couldn't handle doing that, and they needed to bring my husband in and teach him how to give it to me. This was not only true, but I knew that this was the only way I'd get to see my hubby while in the hospital. That evening, Jay arrived to learn how to give me the daily shot of blood thinner I needed because of the blood clots in my body.

When Jay walked into my hospital room, it was like a ray of sunshine flooded my soul. He gently put his arms around me and we held each other and cried. The tears were mixed with all kinds of emotion: relief, love, fear, comfort, sadness, and gratitude. Something about seeing him for the first time made me feel like I was going to make it. When Jay heard about my hospital stay, he was determined to get me home so that he could take care of me himself. We were told the only way that could happen was if I had a trained Registered Nurse at home to check in on me.

Jay and I live in a golf community where everyone's business is everyone's business; the good, the bad, and the ugly. He made a few phone calls and found a neighbor Registered Nurse who was willing to check on me at home. It was late evening, and by this time the attending doctor was starting to get concerned about allowing me to leave. When he found out that Jay had found a home nurse, he wanted to know her name. Well, lo and behold, he had gone to school with our neighborhood nurse Stephanie and apparently was very impressed by her. He finally gave me the ok to go home. Woohoo and Hallelujah!

It felt great to be wheeled out of the hospital and breath the fresh November air. I felt relieved to be going home. Little did I know what steep challenges we were about to face up ahead. I'm so thankful God only lets us see one day at a time. Honestly, that's all I could handle at the moment.

Looking back, I can see that my past had prepared me to face this battle. Having experienced many extreme disappointments and tragedies in my 61 years, God had taught me how to move past victim-mode and into healing. You may ask, "How?"

Stay with me as we explore the rocky path that led to restoration and healing. Do we have to stay a victim for the rest of our lives, or can we rise up and be over-comers? I'm here to say there was and is a way out.

Chapter 2
1962—1970

Calm Years Before the Storm

Sneaking up the spiral staircase with my little 4-year-old legs, I am following the sounds of someone heaving and groaning in pain. The moaning seems to be coming from the guys' dorm at the top of the stairs. I've heard this many times before with some of the other 25 residents who live with my family. But now I want to see it! What does a body look like when it's going through its withdrawals of the addiction to drugs? The smell of our old mansion is stale, and the stairs creak louder than I want them to, as I tiptoe ever so lightly up each wooden stair. I have to be careful that nobody catches me, as I've been forbidden to go up to the guy's dorm. However, this time my curiosity gets the best of me.

9

As I reach the room at the top of the stairs, I see the person in torment. There he is, a teenage boy jerking violently back and forth on a cot. His sweat-soaked body is clutching a thin blanket as he hurls vomit and groans in agony. "Oh God just kill me! Take me pleeease. I don't want to live," I hear him scream.

Wow! I don't ever want to do drugs, I resolve in my little four-year-old mind.

Los Angeles Teen Challenge Center, 1960s

During my early years from 3−10, my dad pioneered and directed the Los Angeles Teen Challenge Ministry which included, a live-in Christian drug rehab home. It was in a large house located in downtown Los Angeles. My two younger brothers, Steve and Rick, lived there with Mom, Dad and me until I was 5 years old. Some of

Andraé at the TC piano

my earliest childhood memories are filled with a lively home of up to 25 residents and my little family living life all together. I watched many young people completely set free from drug addiction and transformed into responsible loving individuals who loved Christ. My life was very affected by the real changes in people's lives that I saw up close and personal during these young, tender years. I couldn't doubt that

God was real after seeing how he worked in the lives of the men and women I lived with.

Every Thursday night there was a chapel service, where dozens of people packed our house. The residents would share testimonies of their life-changing stories and the X-addicts choir would sing soulful gospel songs. The director of the choir was Andre Crouch. He went on to start the world-famous musical group, Andraé Crouch and the Disciples. I was allowed to

Andraé and the Disciples

travel with the group on one of their first tours. We traveled by bus to Canada and held concerts along the way. Every night, Andre, Sherman, Reuben, and Billy sang to packed crowds. It was thrilling and exciting for this little five-year-old girl and impacted my life greatly. I knew that I wanted to be in music ministry, and as God saw fit, that is exactly where I landed later in my life.

My family moved into our own home in Downey, California, when I was five years old. We had a fairly typical "Leave it to Beaver" kind of lifestyle. My youngest brother, Rick, and I played outside on our cul-de-sac with neighbor kids most days. Unfortunately, my brother Steve couldn't join us because of his cerebral palsy. Steve's handicap was caused by a doctor's error in delivery. Steve's speech and walking were affected so that he would never walk or talk normally However, God must have given him an extra dose of optimism because he always had a smile on his face and loved life! (And still does to this day.)

My brother Rick and I attended a Lutheran School down the street for most of my elementary years. Fourth grade was maybe my favorite year. I loved my teacher, Miss Wendy! Our school was not that far from Hollywood. One day a casting crew came to our school to pick some students for the T.V. show called Art Linkletter's House Party. This was a show where 4 or 5 elementary school aged kids would sit on high stools and Mr. Art would simply ask them questions. Of course, "kids say the darnedest things," so the funnier the answer, the more he would egg them on to say more.

The day arrived when they came to my school and interviewed my class. One of the questions they asked was, 'Who takes out the garbage cans in your family?'

My turn finally came, and I answered just as sincerely as I could. I didn't realize at the time that they were looking for funny, not accurate answers. I innocently quipped, "Well it's my dad who takes out the garbage cans. Last week we had a really windy day and our trash cans started blowing down the street while we were eating breakfast. I was like 'Dad, Dad look! Our trash cans are blowing everywhere.' My dad didn't even put any clothes on. He just took off running down the street in his underwear to catch them." Of course, they loved that answer and egged me along so I would give them a blow-by-blow description of my dad running in his underwear. Well, that was it! Apparently, they thought I was funny enough and picked me to go on the show!

The night before the big day of T.V. filming, my mom wrapped my blond hair in little pin curls all over my head. The next day, she carefully sculpted me a fine hairdo complete with hair spray to last all day. It took a little more time than she had anticipated so we arrived a few minutes late. Just as we were pulling into the driveway of the school, the limousine carrying my replacement was actually exiting out the opposite end. I remember being sad about it, but not nearly as sad as my mom. She was completely devastated and blamed it all on herself! She heaved with sobs of sorrow and regret for quite some time. Maybe she believed she had ruined my chances at being a Hollywood star.

When she finally calmed down, she took my little face in her hands and said, "Honey, Mommy is so sorry that I made you late. But I'm going to make it up to you. Today is your day and you can choose anything you want to do. Where would you like to go?" Well of course, where would any 8-year-old American kid living in Southern California want to go? The happiest place on earth of course! So, my mom and I spent an entire day, just her and me at Disneyland. Later, I did get a consolation prize from my substitute...a world globe. Yeah, isn't that thrilling? I'm sure she kept the easy bake oven for herself.

Our family was very committed to our church, Downey Assembly of God. When I was 6 years old, a child evangelist held a kid's crusade there and reenacted the death of Jesus on the Cross. I remember tears streamed down my face when I heard that he would die for me because of my sin. And that if I was the only person on earth, He would still have done it because of how much He loved me. I'm not sure I understood the entire thing, but I remember thinking that if that's how much He loved me, why wouldn't I want to give Him my life? I went to the altar and knelt. With tears I asked Jesus to be my Lord and Savior.

During these wonderful years, God wrote His words onto the walls of my heart. It was the most natural thing to have my young heart focus on believing and loving Him. I hungered to hear His voice and spent much time in sincere prayer. Jesus was alive to me. He wasn't just a story or a picture to color in a Sunday school class. He was a person. He liked it when I talked to Him about my 6-year-

Me with Steve and Rick

old life, and then my 9-year-old heart, and later my 14-year-old self. He listened and spoke back to me. He laughed and cried with me. Not in audible sounds, but in sounds I sensed inside my heart. He was my best friend who accompanied me on the playground, at my desk, and at home.

Secure at Last

Our family was very intertwined with our pastor, Earl Johnson and his family. Pastor Johnson baptized me when I was 6 years old. I could barely see over the baptismal, so he held me up in his arms as I gave my 6-year-old testimony. It was truly a meaningful moment knowing that I was planning to live the rest of my life for Jesus.

Pastor's wife, Darlene was my first piano teacher. I remember wanting to be just like her when I grew up. I was barely 5 years old when I started lessons. We had an old pink beat-up piano outside in the garage. Apparently, I would sit and bang out tunes that I had heard until it sounded like the songs. Our neighbor next door told my mom that if she didn't get a me a piano teacher, she was going to teach me herself. And apparently, she wasn't very good. So, my mom hired Darlene Johnson, the pastor's wife. Through Darlene's classical influence and Andre Crouch's gospel influence, I enjoyed playing many different styles of music. My favorite songs were those with a groove beat, and before you knew it, I was stomping my left foot just like Andre. One of my first performances was at an Audrey Myer concert when I was 10 years old. Little did I know that later down the road, this would become my livelihood.

I want to tell you a little of what it's like to grow up with a handicapped brother. His pain and struggles truly hurt my little girl heart and caused me to become very protective of him. Most people at that time didn't understand people with disabilities. So, he endured a lot of stares and name calling. "Hey retard what's wrong with you? Stop jerking you're getting food all over the place. Can't you move any faster? Hurry up slow poke." People could be so cruel even if naïve. Sometimes it

My parents, Steve, Rick, and me

would make me so angry I would glare right back and call them a few choice names of my own.

Even well-meaning people would pat him on the head and talk down to him with a high-pitched fairy-like voice as if he didn't have a brain at all. However, Steve's cognitive understanding has always been just like yours and mine. Talking down to him made him feel like an idiot. He'd sadly shake his head and tell us, "Why can't people just give me a high five and talk in a normal voice like they do with everybody else? I'm just a person like they are."

I remember a very exciting day when I was seven years old. Kathryn Kuhlman, a famous faith healer was in town and my parents were going to take Steve to the service. My Grandma, Dorothy Hall, was a close friend of Kathryn's so I was sure she would pray for Steve. And in my childlike faith, I was sure he would be healed.

My brother Rick and I were being baby-sat by some family friends that night. I laid in bed for hours and couldn't sleep. My heart was pounding and racing with excitement. I couldn't wait to see him walking or maybe even running; I wasn't sure which, but I was totally sure that he wouldn't be sitting in his wheelchair when he came home. I had heard that many people were healed during these services, and I was sure this would be Steve's night. My childlike faith had no doubts.

When I heard my parents' car pull up, I ran outside fully expecting to see Steve jump out of the car. Instead, I stood there in utter shock. Dad opened the back of the car and got Steve's wheelchair out of the trunk. "What? Why isn't he walking? He wasn't healed?" My little girl faith was completely flabbergasted and dismayed. I couldn't understand why God hadn't healed him when I knew very well that He could. Age old question, right? Why are some people healed and others are not? I can't pretend to know the answer, even now. But hindsight usually gives a person a little better vision and insight.

Looking back, I can see how Steve's sunny disposition has touched many lives. He's been an encouragement to so many others with disabilities and challenges. Quite honestly, he's even been an encouragement to us *normal* people. Because the truth is, we all have *stuff*, inward disabilities that we grapple with. Others may not see them because they are neatly tucked inside us. Over the years, I've heard countless people exclaim, "How can I complain when Steve has so much less than me and lives his life with such joy and optimism?"

One day recently, I asked Steve if he is handicapped in his dreams. His answer completely surprised me. "No, I'm walking and running; no handicaps at all!" I find this totally amazing. And the reality is that he will only have this limited body for a very short time. Soon it will be replaced with a perfectly whole, heavenly body that will thrive for eternity. Despite his circumstances in this limited body, he's a shining example of living with joy. I'm sure this stems from his relationship with Jesus.

My life in elementary school was somewhat similar to the sitcom on television at that time, *Leave it to Beaver*. When I was 9 years old, my dad told us that we were moving to Hawaii to pioneer another Teen Challenge Center. A challenging chapter of my life was about to begin.

Me with my brothers, Rick and Steve

Chapter 3
1970—1976

The End of Pollyanna

I wonder who my best friend will be, is my first thought as I peer around the room of my new 6th grade class in Hawaii. Trying to look relaxed, I smile and try to make eye contact with the brown children sitting around me. I feel a like my tongue is stuck to the roof of my mouth and my body is as rigid as a board. Nobody is smiling back at me. In fact, it looks like they are giving me dirty looks. Feeling very invisible and anxious for a return smile, I try to figure out who looks the least threatening.

Summoning up all my courage. I look at the girl next to me. "Hi, my name is Sherry. I'm new here. What's your name?" To my surprise, she looks over at me and then turns away without a reply. Thankfully the teacher starts to welcome the class before I have a chance to humiliate myself again. Sitting there, the teacher's voice fades into the background as my thoughts swirl around in my head. *There must be something wrong with me; maybe I'm not dressed right; or maybe I need to talk the way they do with that accent; maybe they don't like my blond hair - nobody here has blond hair; or maybe they already have their friends since it's already halfway through the year.*

The bell rings, interrupting my anxious thoughts, and we all file out for recess. Seeing that most of the kids are playing handball, I walk up and stand on the edge of one of the groups. Standing there for an few awkward minutes, I finally ask if I can play. The response of one of the girls is like a slap in the face. "Nah, we no play with haole crap!" Then, to my utter shock, she spits in my direction.

Most everyone's first day of school is a little awkward, but that first day of public school in Hawaii was brutal. I found out that most of these local kids had a true disdain for white kids like me. You might think that *disdain* is too harsh a word, but coming from my vantage point, it was exactly the right word. I was being called "haole (pronounced how-lee) crap" and had no idea what either word meant. When I got home from school, I asked my mom. I'll never forget the details of that conversation. She was taking something out of the freezer when I naively asked her what *haole crap* meant. She looked at me wide-eyed for a second and then sort of swiped at the air like she was going to slap me. "You know we don't talk like that Sherry." My little face must have shown surprised sadness. Realizing that I didn't understand what I had asked, she explained that *haole* was a Hawaiian slang term for white person. And *crap*? "Well, that's basically like dog poop," she explained.

Wow. I remember trying to figure that one out. *Why would they call me that right off the bat without getting to know me? What had I done?* I remember asking myself that question over and over all year long, most of the time accompanied by tears. This was my first introduction to a stigma being attached to the color of someone's skin. Back when I had lived at the Teen Challenge Center in Los Angeles, my daily playmates were the dark-skinned kids who lived in the apartment next door. I literally didn't realize that color was a distinguishing factor in how people might treat one another. I tried to wrap my little head around this new discovery.

I was one of three haole kids in my school. I quickly learned firsthand what it meant to be a minority. One day I was pushed against a wall by some bullies for no apparent reason. *Had I looked at them the wrong way?* I was scared to death as they railed ugly words at me with disgust in their eyes. On another day, I was lifted up and put in a trash can. They might have thought it was funny, but it sure scared the haole crap out of me!

I sat painfully alone at recess and lunch time. My stomach churned with embarrassed sadness because I didn't have any friends. I was blamed for anything that went wrong without anyone to back me up. As the school year plodded along, I began thinking there certainly must be something wrong with me. I just wished I could figure out what it was so I could change it. Why else would they treat me this way? I spent many days walking home from school crying. I didn't understand my new normal, and I sure didn't like it.

We had moved to Hawaii because my dad had been asked to start a Teen Challenge Center there. Initially, it had sounded like a grand idea; sandy beaches, palm trees, and great weather. The five of us packed up our household and said our goodbyes to Los Angeles with visions of a new life ahead. It was 1969, I was 10, and the Hippy movement was in full swing.

We bought a home in a sleepy little community of Kaneohe on the windward side of Oahu. It was set in the gorgeous, lush valley with the Koolau mountains surrounding the community in a semi-circle. Kaneohe is technically in a rain forest, which meant it rained almost every day. The sky would grow dark and heavy, while swollen rain clouds would descend and envelop us. Sometimes we'd get a downpour and sometimes just a sprinkle. When the clouds lifted, we were surrounded by beautiful waterfalls flowing down hundreds of ridges in the mountains.

I loved the beauty of God's creation and would sit staring at the

My brother, Rick, and his surfboard

mountains in awe. It never bored me. Even when I was a child, nature spoke loudly to me of the powerful, creative nature of God. To this day, there is something magical for me about the islands of Hawaii. The warm wet smells of earth and floral scents that blow in the Tradewinds. The damp air filled with the musty smell of wet dirt and the warmth of the sun. The sound of the waves crashing, palm trees rustling in the wind, and birds chirping. For me, there's no place on earth that compares to the magical beauty of the Hawaiian Islands. Whenever I go back, I feel a certain sense of calm relaxation as soon as I get off the plane. It will always be my heart-home.

During the first year there, I spent a lot of time in my room alone and sad. Being a sensitive child, I took the feelings of being rejected and shut out by my peers extremely hard. Coming from a life where I had felt safe and loved, this was an unprecedented painful time for me. There were many occasions where my mom would come into my room and see me crying. She'd sit on the edge of the bed and try to sooth me with comforting words. "Even this too shall pass, Honey. It will pass, and you will look back and see that it didn't last forever." I sorely soaked up the loving encouragement she gave me, even though I wasn't sure she understood the depth of my pain.

I think sometimes we underestimate how much children internalize their early life experiences. Deep and lasting wounds can be forged in the childhood psyche when they experience hurtful situations.

Secure at Last

Without sufficient life experience to draw from, children can easily interpret their hurtful circumstances as being their fault.

I'm not saying this to play the sympathy card. God has truly healed and is still healing that hurt little girl. My point for bringing this up is this: during this period of my life, a *wound button* was formed that would play over again and again when it got pushed. My self-talk went something like this: *Apparently, you were born different from everybody else. You don't fit in because you're not like anybody else. Something is wrong with you. Nobody really likes you. You don't belong.*

Later in life, I realized that this button could be triggered in an instant, and I would react to it in various, precarious ways. I would protect that little wounded child in any way possible. But stay with me here. There was healing up ahead for this little girl. However, it came at a great price. We will talk about that in the following chapters.

That summer my parents knew something had to change. They were losing their happy little girl. They decided that my mom would go to work to help pay for Rick and me to attend a private school. I would be starting seventh grade at Hawaii Baptist Academy. The student body was made up of a mix of white, military kids as well as local kids. This school proved to be exactly what I needed at the time. I began regaining a sense of belonging and started to smile and laugh again. Life returned to a sort of even keel.

Probably because of the fear of not belonging, I joined everything I could. I got involved in the music program, various sports teams, student government, and anything else I could juggle. I joined the handbell choir, played piano, and sang in the vocal choir, cheerleading, and yearbook committee. Once again, I had a circle of friends, and reveled in all

Me with my Hawaiian girlfriend

of the social activities: BBQ's, basketball and football games, beach volleyball, and anything else I could take part in. Anything that fed that little-girl need to belong.

I also got very involved at our church in Kailua. One Sunday evening, Mom was playing the organ when our pastor stopped the singing and asked, "Sherry, would you come up here? We need a piano player tonight to fill in for Tom." We sang choruses that weren't written in music notation or chord charts. We simply played by ear, what we heard in our head. Although I was classically trained, my favorite way of playing was by ear, embellishing a song the way I wanted. Within time, I was enjoying using God's gift of music regularly as the church pianist. I joined a family band of four Tongan brothers from Waimanalo. Our group thoroughly enjoyed playing around the island at weddings and other events.

Because of the Hippy Jesus Movement in the 70's, our church was having an explosive revival. Sunday nights were the *happening* services. They were filled with singing praise and worship songs. After the sermon, there was always a time when people swarmed to the altar, often praying for hours; yes, literally hours. And most of the time, I'd play the piano until the last person left the altar. Many times, it would be close to midnight. Praise and repentance were the center of this revival

My family with Dad's grandma Byrum

movement. Many people gave their lives to Christ during that time, so there was an excitement in the air.

Our Kailua Church was about three blocks from Kailua Beach, so it wasn't unusual to have people wander in dressed in their bathing suits. We welcomed them in one and all. One Sunday night after a service, we hoisted the piano up onto a pickup truck and drove it down to the beach where we could continue singing and sharing the gospel there. We put the piano under an overhanging pavilion. The church members started singing and dancing until quite a crowd gathered around us. The gospel was shared, and people accepted Christ right there on the beach. It was such a great experience that it became a regular event. The church grew in numbers and there was an excitement about Jesus that drew more and more people.

There was a certain urgency about Jesus, even in my own life. I started a habit that lasted for many years. Around 9:00 in the evening, I would spend the last hour of my day reading the Bible, praying, and journaling. God literally met me there. Journaling became the way I could download my feelings, my painful struggles, and questions; the way I wrestled with the voice inside my head that told me, *You're not like everybody else—you're different. You're not good enough. You don't belong.*

Through journaling I learned to hear God speak truth to me. How did He speak? It was kind of like a knowing in my gut. Usually not single words, but just a download of truth. That's what has always separated God's voice from my own. My voice has many words. God's voice is a clear and concise complete thought. It's usually something I would not naturally think of myself.

Here are some additional benefits of journaling:

- Retrospection: seeing both the good to be thankful for, and the bad to learn from and make changes.

- Reveal God's guidance and intervention.
- Reveal missed opportunities to improve awareness in the future.

- Create a record so growth can be noted and embraced.

Secure at Last

I continued to enjoy good friendships throughout high school. One in particular became a very important part of my life in my junior year.

Chapter 4
1975—1977

Little Girls Grow Up to Be Big Girls

Digging my toes into the sand, the hot sun feels like warm fingers massaging my body. My sweaty body is enjoying the break as we rotate teams on the sand volleyball court. The salty ocean air is thick and almost tangible as the waves lap up on the shore with a soft rhythmic beat. *I wish everyday could be a weekend day like this. There is no place I'd rather be than right here playing and frolicking with friends on the beach,* I muse.

As if hearing my thoughts, my best friend Willy kicks sand up on my body and yells, "Get up lazy bones; we've got to get ready for the basketball game."

Secure at Last

A couple hours later, my best girlfriend Cindy and I cheer the boys on to victory against Punahou, our biggest school rival. "Hey can I catch a ride with you to the party," Cindy asks. "You're probably one of the only sober people driving since you're such a teetotaling bore at parties," *she* laughs.

I fake a slap to her head and we both laugh. Cindy continues in a hushed voice. "You know what? Don't tell anybody, but I hope you never change. At least we have someone at the parties who can remember what happens and fill us in later!"

Willy was like a brother, and we shared everything with each other, including our current crushes on guys and girls. We maintained a great friendship and hung out in the same circle of friends. If I had to put a label on our little group, I would say we were the *Jocks* because a lot of our activities revolved around sports. Sometime around our Junior year, Willy and I started looking at each other differently; we started dating. It was a great relationship as dating your best friend usually is. The only problem for me: Willy was not a Christian. A great guy in every other way, but not a Christian.

I thought I could do the missionary dating thing, and that in time, Willy would become a Christ-follower like me. Instead, I started drifting more and more his direction. It was so very gradual and discreet, that I didn't even realize I was changing. That's how Satan tries to lure God's children; one little compromise at a time. Disobedience started creeping in, and before long it wasn't apparent to anyone that I was any different from the group of unbelievers I hung around.

In the summer of my junior year, my pastor's wife, Arlene Shurance, called me aside and asked if I was dating an unbeliever. I was kind of surprised because I hadn't told anybody at church about him. "Yes, I am," I answered. She said that God had given her a warning for me, that if I chose to continue in that relationship, I would eventually walk away from my relationship with Christ. That week, I broke up with Willy with a crushed heart.

Secure at Last

I want to insert right now as I write this, some current, great news: About a year ago, Willy gave his heart to Jesus. While ocean diving a couple miles out in the ocean, he had a heart attack and almost drowned. Taking his last breath, He called out to God, "A little help down here would be great." Just then one of his fins floated over his face, and he was able to get it onto one of his feet and paddle back to shore. That Sunday he attended church. At the end of the service, he made a beeline to the alter and gave his life to Christ. An answer to many prayers over the years. It makes my heart smile every time I think about it.

After the breakup with Willy, I had several supernatural experiences. They all happened at night in my bedroom. I realize that for many of you readers, experiencing the supernatural seems doubtful or even ludicrous. In our country, most people don't ever see into the supernatural realm. Our society has been very influenced by the ancient Greeks, who believed that everything that exists is tangible to us; if we can't experience it, then it doesn't exist. However, people in many parts of the world still hold firmly that we can experience the unseen realm around us. They believe that the unseen world is as real as the seen world.

If you are one that does not believe in experiencing supernatural things in this life, I ask that you give me grace as I recount a few events that happened during this time of my life. We each have experiences in our lives that are hard to explain, and even harder to understand. These are a few of mine.

On a summer night when we were about 16, my friend Lori was spending the night. In the middle of sleeping, I woke up to a voice calling my name, "Sherry." That was all, just my name. Thinking it was Lori, I answered her. She sleepily told me to go back to sleep because it wasn't her. I lay there wondering if I had dreamt it. Again, I heard it loud and clear. This time I knew it was real and it wasn't my friend. I looked under the bed and in the closet thinking someone must be playing a joke on me. The third time I heard my name, I realized this must be God. His voice was calm and loving, but I was shaking and scared, so I asked the voice to go away, and it did. To this day I wonder what I was thinking.

Later that summer I was awakened, and actually saw Jesus coming into my room. Before you think I'm a lunatic and close the book, let me say that right after He left, I wrote the whole experience down in my journal, so that the next morning I would know it was not a dream and had really happened. If you still prefer to think of it as a dream, that's fine, I totally understand.

That night, Jesus came and sat on the edge of my bed and held me in His arms. We spoke back and forth without actual words; somehow, we had perfect communication and I knew exactly what He was saying, a type of telepathy with more clarity than words. I have never forgotten the overwhelming feeling of His ALL-ENCOMPASSING LOVE. It was as if every single part of me down to my cells, the known and the unknown, was completely cherished and oozing with love and acceptance. The love I experienced greatly exceeds even the unconditional love of parents or intimate friends.

I knew that there was nothing about me that wasn't absolutely cherished by Him. It was like nothing I had ever experienced before. Even now as I write these words, I have tears just remembering. Since that encounter, I continue to long for the day that I get to see Him face-to-face and feel that fulfilling love through all of eternity. He loves you exactly like this too!

Speaking of that love, my Great Grandma "Nana" used to talk about the same thing after she had a near death experience. She had clinically died from breast cancer in her 30's and had come back to life with an amazing story. This is what she told me about what happened after she died: "I sped through a tunnel and arrived at a gorgeous garden. Sherry, there were colors and music that I simply can't describe in words because there is nothing like them on this earth. All of nature, the flowers and trees were singing this beautiful music and reflecting the colors through translucent light that bounced off everything. The music was directed to the throne which I could see in the distance. There was brilliant light coming from it and I knew instinctively that this was where God was."

Secure at Last

She was standing at a riverbank. On the other side of this beautiful river, Jesus was standing with His arm outstretched to her. She could hear her daughter, my Granny, screaming and begging God to bring her back to life. My Granny was twelve at the time and quite the hell-raiser. Jesus explained to Nana, "You can come across the river to be with Me, but once you cross over, you can't go back." At that moment, all she could think about was her sobbing daughter, and instantly she was back in her body. She lived many more years but was never fully content being back on earth.

It's interesting how tightly we hold on to life in this body. We live as if this is our final destination and there's nothing after death. However, thousands of people have recounted their near-death experiences. When they return, it seems they have very similar stories about what they've encountered. Life in this body seems very stale and bland compared to their experiences in the next realm. They say it is as if we're living through a veil here on earth. When it is lifted, their new bodies have perfect peace, love, and joy. Their senses are heightened, and they experience heaven in perfectly new dimensions.

Someone who taught me a lot about life and death here on this earth was my best friend, Joy. About five years ago she left this world. I was holding her when she died. She had suffered for two years with stage four pancreatic cancer. Joy had lived her life close to the heart of Jesus. She knew Him intimately because she spent a lot of time talking to Him. Just like most other American women, she loved vacations, parties, new clothes, even spa treatments. Joy and I spent many times together shopping for the perfect treasure at a thrift store, getting manicures and pedicures and lying out in the sun by her pool. You know, all those fun primping kinds of things we girls do with our girlfriends.

While holding her just after she passed away, I looked at the effects of cancer on her pain ridden body. I thought about all the primping we had done to make our bodies beautiful on the outside; and now this frail body looked haggard and worn. It was one of those *aha* moments when I realized that when we die, this world's obsession with looking young and beautiful amounts to nothing. At that point, all that matters is that we have prepared for our new body. Looking at what was left of Joy's frail and empty body, I danced around the room singing with her husband John as she left us to join heaven. Joy was in her forever magnificent body, free from pain.

Please know that I'm not saying we can't enjoy life here, or that taking care of this body is a bad thing. But we don't want to be so caught up in it that we neglect taking care of the most important thing: living with one eye on Heaven. When we lose a person close to us, do we grieve without hope? Or do we rejoice that this life is not all there is? The best is yet to come. I always think of Joy with envy because she got to go on the best vacation of our lives before I did.

I'm so excited to see my Lord and Savior, that sometimes I wish I was there now. However, I know there is a purpose for me to still be here. Each one of us has a purpose. Let's not miss it because we're so caught up in the temporal. God has exciting work for us to do for Him here on this earth – here where we are right now – with the gifts and personalities He's given us. Let's not waste time because there really is a limited amount.

Looking back on that summer of supernatural visitations, I realize now that there was a battle for my soul going on between God and our enemy Satan. I would be remiss if I didn't mention that I was also visited on several occasions by some creatures that I can only identify as hellish. I never saw them. But I felt and heard them. They would usually start at the foot of my bed and start crawling toward me. Somehow, I knew they wanted to choke me.

Their voices sounded like something out of a horror movie. What they said did not make sense to me. They would screech, "Aha, Sherry, Aha," over and over as they crept toward my face. To say I was frightened out of my mind is an understatement. My body would freeze and my mouth would be unable to speak for what seemed like minutes. Each time, I would finally unfreeze and scream out loud "Jesus!" and they would be gone instantly.

Secure at Last

I'm sad to say that during my senior year of High School, I allowed Satan to win the battle for my soul. I turned from God to a full-blown lifestyle that took me far away from Him. My naïve mind wondered what it was like to live like most teens. Part of me was curious and wanted to see what the partying lifestyle was all about.

So, for about a year and half, I joined my friends in their lifestyle. At first it seemed like I had obtained a freedom that was both enjoyable and exciting. My days consisted of playing volleyball on the beach all day and soaking up the sun and surf with friends. Then in the late afternoon, we'd get ready for the downtown Waikiki nightlife. We'd stay out late drinking and dancing through most of the night. As this lifestyle continued, I knew that the things I was doing hurt the heart of God. My heart was sad about that so I shut out the guilty voice in my head. God's voice.

A strange thing happens when we allow other things to take God's place. As time goes by, the things we have been enjoying don't satisfy like they once did. We start replacing them with more extreme acts of disobedience. This was true in my life. In time, I wasn't enjoying the partying lifestyle at all and yet I didn't know how to get out of it. Instead of being free, I was trapped and miserable. The partying I once enjoyed was now not only flat but coming back to bite me.)

Secure at Last

Chapter 5
1978

Crumbling Walls

While driving to Bill's house for a party, my conflicting thoughts are going back and forth. *Maybe I should just turn around and go home. I mean I don't know anybody there except Bill and I barely even know him. Nah, I have nothing else to do; I guess if anything, maybe I'll meet some cool people and have a good time.*

Apprehensively walking into his house, I see that the party is in full swing. People are scattered all over the living room, and the potent smell of marijuana and alcohol fills the air. Bill is on the far side of the room trying to welcome me, but the music is so loud, I can't tell what he's saying. So, I just smile and do a half wave to everybody.

Bill motions me to come sit next to him on a blanket on the floor. As soon as I'm seated, he offers me a joint.

Immediately my mind panics. *Oh shoot, I'm thinking this was not a good idea. These people are wasted. Dang it, why did I come?* But instead, I take the joint and take a couple of light puffs. Pretty soon, people's voices seem to fade in the background and the house takes on a life of its own. The curtains seem to dance to the music, every noise seems amplified in my head, even my breath seems loud. Time seems suspended, and before I know it the people are all gone.

Bill reaches over and starts kissing me. He's a good kisser so I'm somewhat enjoying it. That is, until he starts handling me. "Hey, wait, wait hold on. Let's slow down here." I take his hand and gently push it back. To my surprise, he slowly stands up and starts wrapping me in the blanket we're sitting on.

What in the world is he doing? What the heck? Pretty soon, Bill throws me over his shoulder like a knapsack. Thinking that he's just teasing me, a nervous laugh sound comes out of my mouth. "Stop it, Bill. Hey, put me down you clown," I say trying a little too hard to sound playful.

But instead, he throws me and the blanket on a bed. And then I feel his dead weight drop on top of me. The reality of what is happening suddenly hits me full force, and terror and horror set in. *Oh God NO!!! This can't be happening. Oh, please God make him stop! Why can't I get him off me? Kick harder Sherry, harder!* I feel helpless and immobilized by fear. Even my scream comes out like a choked squeal. My flailing and kicking do not faze him.

The nightmare is happening and there's nothing I can do to stop it! I feel like I'm trapped in quicksand. It's as though my arms, legs, voice, everything, has become useless. Like it isn't my body anymore. It belongs to him.

He's off me now and has walked into the other room. I lay there in utter shock and paralyzed by fear. *Oh God please help me get out of here.* Every part of my body is shaking. I push myself to get up and dress as quickly as my trembling hands will let me. *Can I get to the door safely? Where is he? Will he ambush me again?* I slowly creep to the front door and close it as softly as I can. *There's my VW bug. Sherry, get in the car and lock the door.*

For a while I just sit there stunned, shaking, and crying. My hands gripping the steering wheel, as my head sinks down, and I cry with everything inside me. *What just happened? Oh God, what just happened to me?* The feeling of shame and betrayal, of being taken advantage of and of hating myself for it – so many sickening feelings flood over me.

How am I going to handle this? Just then, this thought came over me, *If I just don't tell anybody, it'll be like it never happened. Yes, that's what I'm going to do. What else can I do? If nobody knows, it will be like it never happened and can't hurt me.*

And that's exactly how I played it out. I told nobody. At that time, I was working at McDonald's as a hostess. My job was to do anything I could to make the patrons happy. Throw a birthday party, lead a store tour, or just walk around and talk to lonely people. I had to wear a "Little Red Riding Hood" outfit that in my opinion looked ridiculous. However, I enjoyed the interaction with the regular patrons. The seating was an outdoor patio with partial covering.

As the weeks went on, I noticed myself sitting a lot more with the customers who wanted to have someone to chat with. They were mostly elderly men who would come in everyday for a hamburger and cup of coffee. They were lonely and loved the attention. When it was quiet, I sat with them, and we'd have a good chin wag. I noticed that I was beginning to sit a little longer, not wanting to get up because of a nagging exhaustion. I was also sick to my stomach. My menstrual cycle had become more irregular than normal, and I had missed a month.

One day a co-worker asked if it was possible; could I be pregnant? I told her there was no chance at all. You see, I wasn't facing the fact that I had been raped. And because I wasn't sexually active, I figured I couldn't be pregnant. When I continued to feel pukey for another couple weeks, my friend took me to the doctor for a pregnancy test. I submitted even though I thought this was probably just a hormonal imbalance.

I'll never forget the exact moment when my doctor came into the room to give me the test results. I was sitting on the table. Without a word, he gave me a big fatherly hug. My heart sank, knowing what he was about to say. He told me the test was positive. I blinked in shock and said that it was impossible. He reiterated that the test was positive and asked me if there had been even one sexual encounter in the last few weeks. I finally admitted to the traumatic rape and exploded in wave after wave of sobs. "This can't be real – please make this not real...." He let me sob into his white jacket.

This man had been my doctor for several years. He proceeded to give me fatherly advice. One thing that still irks me to this day is that he never called the fetus a baby. He said that the embryo inside me was so small that he couldn't even see *it* with a naked eye. He said that he would need a microscope to see *it*.

Looking back, I know that this was a lie, but that his intention was to comfort and help me make the decision he thought was best for me. He said that I was too wounded from what had happened to go through with the pregnancy. He told me that it would be very easy to remove *it*. He also said if I didn't want to tell my parents, I could do the procedure without telling anyone in my family since I had just turned 18, the legal age in Hawaii. My fearful heart clung to his words because I wanted to believe him.

I was desperate for someone to tell me what to do. Today, there is a wealth of information about abortion. There are agencies like Crisis Pregnancy Centers and others that will help a girl go through a pregnancy and the birth of the baby. But in 1978, not much was known about abortion, and I certainly didn't have all the facts to make a wise decision. At this point, I was not only dealing with the reality of the rape but also the reality of a baby from that rape. All I could think about was that a part of Bill, the rapist, was inside me and I hated everything about that. I also thought about my dad's reputation as the Director of Teen Challenge. How could I make him look bad? Another thought that plagued me was how much I didn't want to displease or disappoint my dad. I felt very alone and scared.

After considering everything the doctor had said, I decided to make the appointment for the procedure. My girlfriend who had taken me to the doctor, affirmed my decision. She looked me square in the eyes, and with as much comfort as she could muster, said, "Don't worry about a thing. I'll be with you every step of the way. If you need money, I've got enough to loan you. I can drive you there, so don't worry about that either. And if you don't want your parents to know, just come stay with me for a couple of days; I'll take care of you. Then, when all this is over, you can simply go back to your regular life. I mean, you shouldn't have to suffer anymore. This wasn't your fault."

It all sounded like a welcome relief, so I scheduled the abortion appointment for the following week. In the coming days, so many emotions flooded over me: fear, hatred, self-pity, anxiety, disappointment, confusion, anger, just to name a few. One thought that played over and over in my head was, *Bill made all of this happen and he doesn't have to go through any of this!* The night before the procedure, fearful thoughts raced around and around in my mind. It felt like I was going to explode if I didn't talk to someone.

My brother Rick and I were very close, and I trusted him, so I asked if we could talk in my room. I remember spilling out all of the horrible details of the last few weeks and what I was planning to do the following day. The only thing I didn't disclose was the name of the boy who raped me. I had no doubt that if Rick knew who it was, he would hunt him down and kill him. Surprisingly, Rick thought that I really needed to tell our parents. I seriously disagreed with him at first, but because of his persistent urging, I reluctantly agreed to tell our mom.

I found Mom in the kitchen washing dishes. She looked at me with a strange look on her face. I haltingly started, "Um, hey Mom, when you get done, I have something I'd like to talk to you about. It's private, so could we maybe go for a walk?" With a quizzical look, she nodded, quickly dried her hands, and headed out the front door with me following close behind. I explained the tragedy of a few weeks before, and that I had just had a positive pregnancy test. I reiterated all that the doctor had told me. I paused hesitantly, swallowed hard, and quietly said, "I've scheduled an abortion, Ma. It's for tomorrow. I wasn't going to tell you, but Rick thought it was important that I did."

She didn't respond as I had anticipated. She looked at me strangely again and said, "Sherry, I can't believe you're telling me this. A few minutes ago, when I was doing the dishes, I had a random thought out of nowhere, *what if Sherry was pregnant?* Of course, I dismissed it as a crazy notion, but it wouldn't go away. And then you walked up telling me that you had something important you wanted to talk about. Honey, I can't help but think that God was trying to prepare me for this. So, in a way I guess I'm not shocked, but so incredibly sad that you've gone through all of this without telling me." She hugged me tightly and with tears thanked me for telling her and promised that I wouldn't have to go through this alone. She would be with me.

She told me that no matter what I decided, she would support me. As she saw it, I had three choices:

- I could have the baby and give it up for adoption (her first choice).
- I could keep the baby, and she and dad would support me.
- I could have the abortion if that's what I chose to do.

In my mind, there was only one choice since I hated the person who had done this to me. Consequently, I also hated what was inside me because it was a part of him. Keep in mind that I was an 18-year-old who was far from Christ at that time. I wouldn't make the same decision today, but I do understand the thinking of those who do. I told her that I wanted to go through with the abortion. My wise mama knew it was going to be hard. She told me that she wanted to go with me, and that she wanted the procedure done in a hospital, not an Abortion Clinic.

After the surgery the next day, Mom wheeled me out of the hospital. I'm sure she was praying that we wouldn't run into anyone we knew. Kailua was a small community back in the 70's. Years later I found out how profound an experience this was for my dear mom. She immediately felt guilt and anxiety that she had not taken more time to talk me into a different decision. I'm sad to say that she has lived with this guilt for years. We have both asked each other and the Lord for forgiveness. More about that later.

My initial feeling afterwards was profound relief. The whole thing was over. Maybe now I could have some peace. However, this was not to be the case. For the next few months, I spiraled down a dark tunnel of guilt and shame that eventually led to thoughts of suicide. I felt like a dirty rag that had been tossed aside. Not only did I feel horrible about myself because of my disobedience to God, I also felt disdain for anyone of the male gender. I generally distrusted them and believed that they were all up to no good. That is, of course, except for those in my family who I trusted.

About a year later, I had gone on a date to see a movie. During one of the scenes, there was a depiction of a dark hole in the ground. All you could see were the hands of tiny babies reaching out from the bottom of a pit. They were screaming at their mothers who had aborted them and cut their life short. "Why? Why?" they screamed at their mothers. My heart pounded wildly, and my head felt like it was going to spin off. For the first time, I was confronted with the fact that I had killed a baby; I had killed a human being. I immediately asked the guy I was with to take me home. I shook all over on the drive, and no matter what he said, I couldn't be consoled. That poor guy never knew what happened to his date that night. I suppose he suspected.

All the feelings I had suppressed about the rape and abortion welled up to the surface and overwhelmed my whole being. I was so angry! Angry at everyone, but mostly the one who had raped me. He had taken so much from me, my innocence and carefree life. He had caused so much pain and he himself didn't have to face any of the consequences. I was left with the shame, the guilt and sorrow from the abortion. I felt so broken inside. I had messed up so badly that I thought even God had forgotten about me, and that whatever purposes He had desired for my life had been crushed to nothing.

I was also incredibly angry at myself. What kind of person was I to take an innocent baby's life? I was deplorable and was sure that even God Himself had turned His back on me. I was far from that little girl who had felt loved and adored by Jesus just a few short years ago. I had made a broken mess of my life and wasn't sure there was anything good left to salvage of it. I mourned for the baby that I had taken out of this world. What kind of life would this child have had? I would never know. He or she wouldn't ever have a chance at life because of my selfish decision.

One day when I was particularly down, I went into my parents' bedroom and laid face down on the floor. I cried until I couldn't cry anymore. I wanted to die, but I thought I would go to hell and that terrified me even more. In my mind, there was absolutely no hope for me at all. I felt trapped in a tunnel with no light at the end, a prison of horrible anguish that I couldn't escape. I seriously thought that I had committed the unpardonable sin and had gone even too far for God's forgiveness. I don't know how long I lay there before my dad walked in and saw me.

His reaction took me by complete surprise. Instead of showing disappointment, he lovingly helped me off the floor and sat me next to him on the edge of the bed. "Sherry honey, it's ok. I know what happened. Your mom shared it with me. And it doesn't matter what you have done or what you'll ever do, I will always love you; I will always forgive you. Don't you see, Honey, that nothing can ever change my love for you? And God's love is so much greater than even my human love. If I as your earthly father can love and forgive you through any pitfall, how much more will your Heavenly Father welcome you back with open arms. His love is perfect. It's not fickle. It doesn't change with your ups and downs. It's constantly the same. He is faithful even when you're not!"
I literally do not have words to describe what that moment did for me. It had a huge impact on my life because I was so afraid of disappointing my dad, God, and everybody else. For the first time

in a year, I felt the possibility of hope. The dark tunnel now had a small crack of light at the end of it. Maybe there was still grace to be forgiven by God and have a future with Him. I didn't imagine that I could ever be completely healed from all the garbage, but maybe, just maybe, I could "eat the crumbs from the floor" like the prodigal son story in the Bible.

If you've never read the story of the prodigal son, I urge you to read it. It's in Luke 15:11–32. The story is about a son who greedily asks for his inheritance before his father dies. The father grants that request, and the son goes off and parties until all his money runs out. When he is so destitute that he feeds pigs for a living, he begins to eat the very food the pigs eat. He thinks back to the good old days when he was with his wealthy father. He returns home so he can ask if he can just be one of his father's servants since he knows he's not worthy of more than that. Instead, he sees from afar, his father running towards him. The father not only forgives and accepts him but tells him that whatever wealth he has will be shared with his son. The father throws a big party for him saying, "My son was lost and now he's found."

For those of us who have children, we can say that we would love and support our kids through anything. Yet our desire for our kids is only a faint echo of God's great love for each of us. The amazing thing is that His extravagant and infinite love is unconditional NO MATTER WHAT WE'VE DONE. Maybe you think that you're too far gone for God to accept you. Please know that no matter what you've done or where you are in life, God's love for you has never changed. It's forever and it's unconditional.

When I started to believe that my Heavenly and earthly father loved me unconditionally and would forgive anything I had done, I again asked Jesus to be my Lord and Savior. I remember telling Him that even if I never *felt* His presence again, I would completely give my life to Him, and obey whatever He told me to do. This was different from my first conversion when I was a child. It was much more of a choice, and not based on a feeling.

That choice was tested; I didn't *feel* God for many months. I had to live my life for Him by choice. I was choosing to follow a God that I could not see, and for the most part, couldn't even sense. But I knew it was the right choice because it was truth.

I was unprepared for how slow the process was going to be in rebuilding my relationship with God. I thought that somehow, I would be back in the same intimate relationship I had with Him before. But, the stony coldness of my heart melted more slowly than I expected. My fallenness had trapped me as habits and attitude patterns had woven their tentacles around my heart. I felt devoid of the warm and spiritual vitality I had enjoyed for most of my life. Sin has a way of stealing our soul, and during this rededication I wasn't sure my decision would survive.

There were tearful times of repentance and confession. Sometimes I felt unable to believe again for fear of what He might say to me. The dirty mess of what I had allowed my life to become made it hard to see clearly. But as time passed, I saw Who was standing there waiting for me. Jesus wanted to take all the heaviness and weariness away from me. I slowly began to trust Him again.

He hadn't abandoned me. He had been there all along. It was sin that had blinded my eyes and dulled my heart. I began to hear His quiet voice once again. He desired to heal me, to give me a future and a hope; to heal the layers of my thinking. There were secret areas that He wanted to touch with His Spirit. With my hand in His, we could rebuild a new future for His glory. I had come back home.

Since my friends at the time lived their lives for themselves and not for God, I decided it would be good to get away from their influence. I had to be literally removed from one environment and deposited into another for the destructive routines and habits to be broken. I reached out and asked my Granny if I could come stay with her for a while. She lived in Southern California, and I thought that was far enough from Hawaii to start a do-over.
I lived with my Granny for about three months, gleaning from her infinite patience and wise Christian counsel. However, there were some deep-rooted attitudes from the hurts I had encountered that

needed some in depth counseling. I decided to go to a Discipleship Training School in Hawaii with an organization called Youth with a Mission (YMAM). This was a 6-month live-in school that taught you in depth how to be a disciple of Christ. Emphasis was placed on getting to know God and becoming the person He created you to be. Each student was assigned a counselor.

Secure at Last

Chapter 6
1979

A Radical Complete Healing

Tiptoeing to my counselor Gail's little cottage, I hope I don't wake anybody up. I've had yet another nightmare involving a man. It's usually a man I don't know and his acts on me are violent. Tonight's dream was rather intense, and I woke up in a pool of sweat. *I just need to talk to somebody, and Gail told me that she's here to talk with me day or night. Hopefully she means that!*

Gail opens the door with her nightgown on and looks at me with her sleepy eyes. I find myself stammering all over myself. "Oh Gail, I'm so sorry! I probably shouldn't have come over. Go back to sleep. I'll just come back in the morning." I turn around so as not to make eye contact with her sleepy eyes anymore.
"Nonsense Sherry, come on in and have a seat on the couch. I'll put the tea kettle on." Feeling rather awkward I walk in, find the couch

and sit while she goes to the kitchen, which isn't far away. She continues to talk. "Honey, you look like you've seen a ghost. Did you have another nightmare?"

The words start to tumble out as I recount the strange man who brutally attacked me in my dream that night. I begin to weep. "Gail, I hate men. Most of them are such scum bags. You know, I don't think I will ever let a man get close to me again. I seriously don't trust them!"

I'm expecting a reprimand from Gail, but instead she sits right next to me on the couch and takes me into her arms. As I ugly cry, Gail just holds me, patting my back ever so gently. "Why Gail? Why did this have to happen to me? And why do I keep having these dreams? Is this going to haunt me for the rest of my life? I don't want to hate men, but I can't help it!"

I pull back and look deep into her eyes for answers. Peering back at me with only love she says, "Honey, Jesus hates what happened to you and is deeply saddened by what happened. He understands your anger and distrust of men. But He wants you to be healed and set free from this hatred and unforgiveness because the truth is, it is only hurting and crippling you. He wants to heal you so that someday you can have a healthy relationship with a good man who loves you."

"Oh Gail, I don't believe I will ever be healed from this hurt. I want to, but I just don't know how it could ever happen."

"Well, I believe that you can be completely healed, but only if you really want to be."

"Of course, I do," I say a little quicker and sharper than I intend. Why this makes me irritated I don't know.

Undeterred, Gail gently continues. "I know you do, Sweetheart. And if you're willing, I want to lead you in a healing prayer. But this is not just a one-time prayer. It's the start of a prayer that you and I will be engaging in for a while. Jesus and I will walk with you through this until you have received a new and healed heart."

"What? Really? Yes, yes! I want this so bad! Do you think we can start tonight?"

"We sure can. Let's do that right now."

Gail had me walk through the night of the rape, recounting every emotion as I talked it out. She told me that Jesus had NOT left me alone that night. He was right there beside me. She had me visualize Jesus by my side through the entire event, and the subsequent days that followed the rape.

I also spoke out every lie that I was believing about myself during that time; that I was dirty, undeserving of good treatment, powerless, and alone. Then, she had me verbalize the truth about my situation: that I was a cherished daughter of God, worthy of respect, powerful in Christ, and definitely not alone! Jesus was right there with me!

Let's pause right now and turn the spotlight over to you. Can you think of any lies that you have believed about yourself? Lies that maybe play over and over in your mind? Lies that make you feel insecure or less than others and keep you bottled up with fear or lack of confidence? Maybe nobody knows about them because you've hidden them so well. Yet you find that when certain things happen in your life, the lies play out in your head.

Can you think of what that trigger button may be that causes you to react with fear, anger, or sadness? Can you think back to a situation or situations, even way back in childhood, that might have started those awful feelings? And even more importantly, can you pinpoint the lies that you began to believe about yourself after it happened?

I encourage you to take some quiet time to search your heart. It might be good to take paper and pen, and honestly ask yourself the above questions. We've all had painful experiences and it is truly amazing how much the hurts and lies we were left with can control us. The good news is, they can be pinpointed and healed, through Jesus and His truth. I know because He's healed me of a lot.

Gail also encouraged me to forgive each person who had hurt me

King's Mansion – our DTS base

by speaking out loud, as I relived these hurtful circumstances. She told me that forgiveness was not a feeling but a choice. As we walked through each hurtful situation, I said out loud, "I forgive you, _____." She told me that each time that person came to mind, I should pray for them, and reiterate that I had forgiven them. Not because they were right, but because unforgiveness *only hurt me*. When I forgave, it unhooked me from the unforgiveness that tied me to the other person. Forgiveness set me free.

Gail said that when it would be helpful, I should make amends with the people who had hurt me. Of course, that wouldn't be appropriate for the rapist, or the kids in my elementary school who taunted me. However, there was one relationship that I needed to make amends. My father. You see, growing up, I had felt unimportant to him due to his long work hours. I missed him and wished we were closer. It was clear that I needed to have a conversation with him. I remember gathering as many quarters as I could and calling him from a payphone, where they now lived in northern California.

When I shared with him how I felt, I could tell he was shocked. He had no idea I felt unimportant to him. He told me that was the farthest thing from the truth. He was just doing what men did at that time; work hard and provide a good living for their families. There were many tears, and from that day on, we have worked to make our relationship stronger. I am so grateful for the wonderful relationship we enjoy today.

When we confront darkness with light, the light wins. When we confront unforgiveness with forgiveness, forgiveness always wins. We can truly be free to walk through life as a whole individual, not burdened down with the lies we once believed. Jesus sets us free with TRUTH and FORGIVENESS!

I have talked with many women who have been raped and or had abortions that are still being affected by the pain and effects. It breaks my heart, knowing that there is hope and freedom for them if only they apply these principles. I'm not saying it's easy—believe me it's NOT. Is it worth it? YES. If living a happier and more purposeful life is there for the taking, why wouldn't we choose this road?

Many cannot do this alone. I encourage you to seek out and find someone who understands these principles and can help you apply them. I am living proof that one can be completely healed. As you read on, you will see that I have had to apply these principles to other circumstances again and again. We all get hurt, because life is complicated. But there is HOPE.

Another teaching in YWAM that impacted my life greatly was called *listening prayer*. We usually think of praying as asking God for something. At least I always did. However, in 1 John 5:14-15 it says, *This is the confidence we have in*

In my beloved Hawaii again

approaching God: that if we ask anything according to His will, He hears us. And if we know that He hears us - whatever we ask - we know that we have what we asked of Him.

Ok, so when we pray God's will, we have what we ask. I had never thought about asking God what was on His heart and what He wanted me to pray. Couldn't God just do what He wanted to do without me praying?

I learned that God created us to partner with Him in this world. To be His companion. He wanted to share creation and life with each of us. Could it be that God wanted you and me to partner with Him to see His will accomplished in this world? What a humbling design for failed humanity. And yet, if true, what an amazing offer of relationship Christ has handed each one of us.

I must be honest. I always thought that God's will was to make me happy. That's not true. It's what American Christianity teaches, but that's not what the Bible teaches. His will is to see us be transformed into His likeness and to teach others to do the same. I found out that when I quieted myself and listened for God's small voice to tell me what He wanted to accomplish in my life and in the lives around me, my prayers became powerful. I began to see God do amazing things.

So how did it work in our prayer time in YWAM? We would spend some time worshiping God together. That would define how great He is and how honored we are to partner with Him. Then, we'd ask God to cleanse us from any sin that came to mind. And then we would quiet our voices and listen for God to speak what was on His heart. We would try to align ourselves with His will rather than convincing God that what we wanted was a good idea. Sometimes I had a hard time keeping my mind focused on Him for the full fifteen minutes. But like anything, with practice it became easier, and I began to recognize and know what His voice sounded like.

Sometimes, it would be like a puzzle. Each person had their own piece, a word from God, a scripture, a vision, or even a song. And when we put it all together, these pieces formed a clear picture of what God wanted to say to us, and how He wanted us to pray. It was beautiful, and we saw many answers to prayer, which I will embellish on later.

There was a lot of teaching on repentance and changing habit patterns. One night after a teaching like this, everyone began to pray and ask God to show them areas in their lives where they needed to repent. As time went on, it became quite loud as people began to feel the Holy Spirit point out sin in their lives. There was a lot of weeping and confessing; including myself as I was made aware of areas of disobedience.

I'm not sure how to describe what happened next, except to say that it felt like I was taken away from the room to a different place. It was a beautiful garden. I couldn't hear the crying anymore. It felt like giant hands came from the sky and took hold of my hands. They started spinning me around and around until I was off the ground, kind of like a dad does when he swings his kids around in circles. We were laughing and enjoying one another as a daddy and daughter would.

I'm not sure how long I was *in* that garden before I could hear the crying in the room again. Right then, God spoke clearly to me and said "My daughter this is what I desire. When you ask forgiveness, you don't have to stay there and wallow in pain feeling horrible about yourself. As soon as you ask, I forgive you so that we can be back in close relationship and enjoy each other again." Wow! That was quite a revelation.

God was more interested in enjoying me than seeing me remain sad about my sin. My natural tendency was to hold on to the guilt and shame for a long time. But God was telling me that once I confessed my sin, it was gone. His desire was to enjoy our relationship. Have you ever thought about the fact that God created us to enjoy relationship with Him? That's the purpose of us being created here on this earth. Maybe we should ask ourselves: How much do we actually do that?

DTS classmates and staff

When we finished the first three months of training at Youth With a Mission, I felt stronger than I had ever been, and ready to embrace the next part of the DTS, a three-month outreach. The team I was assigned to had only 15 people: six girls, six guys, a leadership couple, and a baby. We were going to the Hawaiian island of Maui to reach out to the community with Jesus' love. We lived on Front Street at the end of downtown Lahaina. The house had only two bedrooms. In the girl's room there were triple bunk beds across from each other and a porta crib for the baby in the corner. The leadership couple stayed in the other bedroom. This left the 6 guys out in the chicken coop, which we converted into somewhat of a bedroom.

Our team was extremely poor. Most of us had spent all of our money on the tuition and airfare to Hawaii. We often ran out of food. But, remember we were taught to listen to God's heart, and then pray right? We did a lot of that for the next three months. And God answered our prayers in the most curious of ways so that we would know that it was most definitely His provision! The examples that follow are not at all embellished and are 100% true.

One day as we had finished praying for food, a lady knocked at our door. She had a car full of grocery bags full of food. She told us that God had spoken to her and told her that she was to bag up her pantry and bring us as much food as she possibly could. Apparently, this lady really loved God, because she even stopped at the store and bought more on her way over.

Another day during our listening-prayer time, one of the guys told us that God impressed on him that we should go down to the harbor and wait. As we were seriously down on food, we were willing to do whatever it took. We all walked down Front Street to the harbor and stood there expectantly for a while. When nothing happened right away, we were feeling somewhat awkward. After a while, a boat pulled up to the dock. The fishermen from the boat began unloading fish. At one point, one of them came up to us and said, "Hey, do you guys want a Wahoo fish? We caught so many, we don't have room for them all." We couldn't have been more gratefully surprised. We thanked him profusely and told him he had been part of a miracle. I'm not sure he really grasped the enormity of the situation. But we knew that God had provided once again.

One of my favorite answers to prayer was when God used me during a prayer time. I literally had a picture of hot dogs and ice cream float through my mind. *That was strange*, I thought, *I must be hungry*. When it was time to share what we had heard, I told them about my *vision* of hot dogs and ice cream. We all had a good laugh and thought that maybe I had fallen asleep and just dreamed a crazy dream.

Later that evening, we received a phone call from a small mom-and-pop business down the street. They said they were closing for good and wanted to know if they could bring us a surplus of food that they were trying to get rid of quickly. Guess what kind of business it was? You betcha, a hot dog and ice cream store!

Living on hot dogs and ice cream was yummy for a while but can play serious havoc on a girl's figure. So, a couple weeks later, we started praying for food that was less fattening. Not long afterwards, we received a phone call from a prominent restaurant in town with a huge salad bar. They wanted to know if instead of throwing away their salad bar every night, they could bring it to us. We were simply amazed that God would concern Himself with the little things that mattered to us.

Lunch at King's Mansion

The last miracle I want to tell you about had to do with my friend Pam, from Buffalo New York. She was a little bubbly spitfire who wore glasses that looked way too big for her face. She told us that God had revealed to her that He wanted her to go on to the next school in YWAM, the School of Missions. She had put her application in, even though she realized her bank account was empty. We prayed long and hard for Pam to receive the money she needed for the tuition. Each day we asked Pam if she had gotten any letters with money inside, and each day the answer was "no." This went on for several weeks until it was down to the last day for her to make the deposit to secure her spot in class.

This time when the mail came, we all walked to the mailbox with Pam holding our breath expectantly. There were two letters for Pam. Our faith was so sure that we all shouted, "This has to be it." We watched expectantly as she opened the first letter, and there was a check in it. She read us the amount and it was about one third of what she needed. Our hearts sank.

Then she opened the second letter and...there it was...a reimbursement for an insurance bill that she had overpaid several months ago. The amount? Exactly the other 2/3 that she needed for the school deposit. In fact, almost right down to the very dollar. I will never forget our reaction. We all fell into one big heap of hugs and laughter.

You can see now why I had so much faith in God's provision when I left the DTS in Hawaii. I felt recharged and ready to move back to California. I had been taught many helpful tools that brought me from pain to healing.

In summary, the tools were:

- *Revisiting the hurtful situation and picturing Jesus lovingly standing with me, knowing that I wasn't alone.
- *Forgiving the person/people who hurt me. More about that later in the book.
- *Pinpointing the lies that I believed about myself because of the situation.
- *Replacing the lies with the truth of what God says about me in the Bible.

Full disclosure: As you will see in the remaining pages, there were many times that I walked through the darkness of pain. Sometimes it took time before I was ready to let go of the pain and use these tools for healing. But I can honestly say that whenever I decided to put these tools into practice, God was faithful to restore me back into a joyful and healthy woman.

Chapter 7
1979—1981

Teacher: Ms. Hall

"Ok that's it! I'm sick and tired of you guys horsing around and not listening to me! Go ahead, but I'm not going to stand up here and pretend to teach when nobody's listening!" As I dramatically turn around and head for the door to leave these sassy 6th graders, I hear a student shout out.

I turn around to see Fonzie (at least that's what I call him) jump up in front of the classroom of students. "Shut up and sit down," he shouts! And low and behold every one of those students sits down in their seats and quietly comes to attention.

I slowly make my way back to the front of the class and emphatically say, "Ok that's better! So, if you're done now, let's continue where we left off. Johnny, how many beats does a whole note get?" I now have their undivided attention thanks to Fonzie.

For those of you who don't know who Fonzie is, he's the character that played the cool dude in Happy Days, a popular sitcom in the 70's and 80's. All the kids in the school looked up to him because he was taller and older than the rest of them. This was the case with my Italian student, Lorenzo. He was probably 2 years older than the rest of the class and at least a head taller. He had a bit of a mustache and a beard that he was mighty proud of. Lorenzo was every girl's dream and every boy's nightmare.

However, much to Lorenzo's shame, at his 6th grade graduation, his Italian mama outed him in front of the entire class. "Miss Hall, you know why my son always stick up for you? He think you da most beautiful woman he ever see!" It was the one and only time I saw a crack in Lorenzo's armor. He actually looked flustered!

I had just finished a semester at Bethany Bible College in Santa Cruz, California. My folks had moved from Hawaii to Pastor at Milpitas Calvary Assembly of God near San Jose, California. During the long Christmas break, I stayed with them, attending their church and College Class.

At the end of Christmas break, the school affiliated with my dad's church asked if I would teach K−8 grade music. They also wanted me to direct their school choir and coach the girl's cheerleading squad. It was an offer I couldn't turn down. I was going to Bethany to become a music teacher, and here I was being offered that very job. It felt like a perfect opportunity.

I absolutely loved my new job. Music had always been my second language, and I found that I also loved teaching. Teaching a music curriculum to various age groups was a challenge that I found thoroughly enjoyable. I had been giving private piano lessons since I was 16, but this was a fun segue. My favorite age group was third through fifth graders. I loved this age because they were old enough to learn new concepts, but young enough to still think that their teacher was up in rank next to God.

I also taught the school choir, consisting of about 150 kids. On special holidays, we would put on musical performances. This was back in the day when most people didn't use cordless microphones. I pretty much had to use my yelling voice throughout the rehearsal times. Just before the Christmas performance I happened to come down with a cold. My already overused vocal cords were now being attacked by a virus. However, the show must go on, right? After the performance was over, I was left with a squeaky raspy voice that sounded a lot like Rod Stewart. Not attractive for a young woman. Getting any words to come out took all my energy.

By this time, it was winter vacation, and time to take my girls to their cheerleading camp. There is a lot of screaming in a cheer camp, from sunrise to sundown. As their coach, do you think I wasn't going to participate? I honestly don't remember whether we won the cheer competition that year, but I do know that I gave my vocal cords another harsh beating.

Returning home, I didn't have any voice at all. After a few weeks, it didn't seem to be healing and was affecting my teaching and everyday life. When someone is a talker and their voice is taken away, it's a hard pill to swallow. When I finally decided something was clearly wrong, I went to see a doctor. X-rays revealed that I had polyps on my vocal cords—not a good diagnosis for a teacher or anyone who loves to talk. He told me that my choices were:

• To have surgery, which could have an adverse effect on my speaking and singing voice.

• To stop talking completely for three months.

• To reduce talking for six months.

I didn't want to damage my speaking and singing voice, so number 1 was out. Completely giving up talking for three months seemed virtually impossible. So, I chose number 3: reduce talking for six months. If you think reducing your talking is not hard, try hanging around your friends and just listening. Think about it, just listening. For some of you, that might sound like a lovely respite from the noisy world we live in. But for my type A personality, this was an excruciatingly hard task.

I learned that if I used a notepad and pen, sometimes I could get my two cents in the conversation. I would write what I wanted to say, and then ring a bell so the person/people could read it. Sometimes they would stop the conversations and read it, but many times they just ignored me. It all seems humorous now looking back. One thing I learned during this time of silence was how few people, including myself, really listen to what others say. I noted that most people were just busy formulating what they were going to say in response, and then looking for a break in the conversation to jump in.

People seemed quick to interrupt others to get their point across. That's probably why the Bible says in James 1:19 NIV, "Everyone should be quick to listen and slow to speak." Real listening is an art, and one that we should all be striving to practice. People feel valued and loved when they are heard.

It was during this time of forced silence that I met my husband-to-be. What a shock for him when my voice came back a few months later!

He was and still is a professional gospel singer. His singing career started at a young age at a mega church in Southern California. Later he became the lead singer in a famous gospel singing group. When I met him, he was traveling and singing solo for churches and different events. He was a regular on the Christian Broadcasting Network on TV as well as other television networks.

Chapter 8
1981—1984

Marriage and Family 101

"Can the piano player please come back up and accompany me on a song?"

I'm sitting in the back row of church with a football player named Ralph who I had invited to go to church with me that day. When I get up to the piano, Rusty, the special singer that day, whispers in my ear, "Hey would you be able to play the song *Great is Thy Faithfulness*?" Of course, this is an old hymn I know well, so I begin playing as he sings each verse through to the end. He finishes the service with a prayer, and I get up and start to leave. But not before Rusty intercepts me at the piano.

"Hey, I couldn't help but notice that we play well together," he says. "Would you be open to playing for me when I do concerts in this area?"

'Sure, that sounds good," I respond. We exchange phone numbers; say our niceties and I head to the back of the church where I left Ralph sitting. I need to get him outside to the lobby so I can introduce him to some of my friends in the single's group. I want him to meet them before we head over to the barbecue.

As I whisk past my dad in the lobby, he reaches out and touches my arm. "Hey honey, can I steal you for a second?"

Wondering why he wants to talk to me alone, I follow him into his office.
"Hey, Sweetie, do you have any plans for lunch? Mom and I are taking Rusty out and it sure would be great if you could come along with us." He has that determined look in his eyes that I have seen many times before when he has an agenda.

"Uh, no, can't today, Dad. I brought a football player from college to church today. I've got a picnic lunch at the park planned for our single's group, so he can meet some other Christians."

I can tell right away that dad is not happy with that answer. He persists, "You know, Sherry you just have to start meeting the right kind of guys if you intend to marry a good man. Rusty is in the ministry and a solid Christian man. Can you possibly change your plans?"

"No, sorry Dad. The picnic is already set up and the ball player is waiting for me in the lobby."

"Ok. But I sure wish you'd reconsider." His jaw is tight, and his temples are slightly pulsating.

I was 20 years old, and thoroughly enjoying singleness with some great friends at my dad's church. We had a very active college group where I met lifelong friends. To this day, we revert to being 20-year-olds whenever we see each other at reunions. That day, I had no idea that my singleness was about to abruptly change.

My first impression of Rusty was that he was another of those performers who was a little "too polished and perfect; and maybe a little full of himself," so it didn't bother me that I had plans. Plus, I was doing God's business in bringing a new Christian to church. A funny back story about the football player was that I had taken him to a Billy Graham crusade that very week. He had asked me to go down to the altar with him to give his life to Christ. Somehow that night on the local news, there was a clip of Ralph and me going down to the altar. At school that week, I had been razzed about it by my teacher friends. "Oh, Miss Hall, we're so glad you finally gave your heart to Jesus." It was actually pretty funny.

Rusty called soon after that Sunday service and we had an enjoyable chat. I was a bit surprised to find out that we had so many things in common despite a thirteen-year age difference. We both grew up in a Pentecostal church and gave our lives to Christ at a young age. Our families were both very important to us and we had enjoyed a normal healthy childhood. Music was an integral part of who we were and what we wanted to accomplish in our lives. We had a similar sense of humor and enjoyed doing many of the same things. If it weren't for the age difference, I probably would have given some thought to dating him.

Rusty continued to phone periodically, and we chatted away for hours. I thought of him as a big brother. I remember telling my best friend Marta that I enjoyed our conversations and wished that he wasn't so much older than I. Rusty and my Uncle Dave had been friends in college when I was six years old. He remembered a day when Uncle Dave had brought him to our house to do laundry. I told him that I didn't remember because I was probably up in a tree or playing hopscotch. We both laughed.

One day he asked if I'd be interested in flying down to Southern California to accompany him at a large Christmas Banquet. He said he'd pay my airfare and expenses. I had two weeks off for Winter Break, so I agreed.

Secure at Last

My Granny lived a few miles from Rusty, so I arranged to stay with her. The day before the banquet, Rusty called and asked if I could meet him at his apartment to practice and spend the day with him. I had no idea at the time how this one day would change my life! There was a ski show nearby at the Anaheim Convention Center, so we started our day there. As we were walking around the arena, Rusty reached over and took my hand. I was completely blind sighted. A myriad of feelings swirled in my head. I had only thought of him as a big brother type of friend. For heaven's sakes, he had gone to college with my Uncle Dave. A barrage of thoughts flooded my mind. *What is he doing? He's too old for me. Do I like this? What does this mean?*

Eventually, we went back to his apartment to practice, and it was there that he gave me the first kiss. Ok, so now I knew what he was up to. But did I like it? We were sitting on the piano bench when he asked if I would mind if he kissed me. I teasingly replied, "Um, I don't know, let me pray about it and see what God says." After a pause I said, "Ok, He said, yes." I know they say you can't fall in love in an instant, but obviously they weren't talking about us. From that moment on, we were both fully engaged in this new relationship.

Rusty's sisters

The next night was the Christmas banquet. It was in a *fancy* hotel in downtown Anaheim. I'm talking about crystal chandeliers, white tablecloths, and women dressed in fancy gowns with diamonds. Rusty wanted me to wait with him outside to welcome his sisters. He was so excited to introduce them to me that when he saw them coming up the hotel driveway, he ran out the double doors shouting, "Here they are."

As soon as I saw Cherie and Cindy step out of their white Mercedes, I was blown away. Never had I felt more like a beach hillbilly. Walking up were two gorgeous blonds coifed in fur coats, red lipstick, and stiletto heels. Remember, I was a simple island girl whose sense of dressing up was simply not to wear flip flops.

62

However, all my self-consciousness faded as soon as they smiled and reached out to give me a hug. I could tell that they were sweet down-to-earth, good-hearted people and I instantly liked them.

That night was a whirlwind with Rusty introducing me to one person after another. Just before we preformed, I snuck away to the eggnog bar to catch my breath. Noticing a girl literally shaking as she poured her eggnog, I asked if she was ok. With eyes gleaming she responded, "Yes, but I can't stop shaking. I just talked to Rusty Peavy." I couldn't help but laugh and she asked me if I was there as a member of the Singles Group at Melodyland. When I explained that I was there to play the piano for Rusty, I thought she was going to choke on her eggnog. She looked at me with wide-eyed wonder and envy. Of course, I played this up all night telling Rusty how honored I was to be playing for the world-famous Rusty Peavy. And of course, I had to say it the way she did, with my eyelashes fluttering.

As he and I spent the next few days together we realized that what we were feeling was something special. I extended my trip another week in order for us to have more time together. When I arrived home three weeks later, I was walking on clouds and everybody that saw me knew I had been smitten. Mom instantly knew that this was different from any other guy I had ever dated. Dad was thrilled.

Two months later, Rusty drove me to a beautiful ocean front condo. The aroma of Orange Baked Cornish Hen, scented candles, and fresh flowers met me as I walked through the front door. The patio door was slightly open and the sounds of the ocean waves combined with the smooth jazz playing in the room completed a perfect romantic dinner.

It was then that Rusty asked me to marry him. But literally before I could get the words out of my mouth, the lights in the whole building suddenly went out. No kidding, darkness except for the glow of the candles. Yes, there had been a power outage!

I picked up on the moment and quipped, "Uh oh, is this a sign?" Of course, my response after that was a hearty yes!

Secure at Last

We were married four months later at Dad's church, followed by a second wedding at Melodyland where Rusty attended, so that his friends in Southern California could attend. The year was 1982. Rusty was almost 35 and I was 22. We enjoyed a honeymoon traveling up the California coastline stopping at Disneyland, the beach, The Madonna Inn, and some other fun destinations.

Shortly afterward, Rusty and I headed to Britain for a 3-month tour with evangelists Paul and Lucille Cantalon. They were the speakers, and we provided the music at churches across England, Scotland, and Wales. We had booked this tour pretty tight with services every single night. For the first two months, we literally had 60 services in 60 days. I think even God was tired of church at the end of that grueling schedule. I know we were!

During the days, we hung out with the families who were hosting us. They took us on tours of the cities and introduced us to their culture. I loved getting to know the history and listening to their accents. However, I didn't like the lack of heating in their modest homes. Most of the houses we stayed in didn't have central heating. We were usually given a rubber hot water bottle to ease the damp, biting chill. That lasted all of about fifteen minutes. The only heat we had was the heat we could generate from each other's bodies. That led to a lot of rearranging single beds and a lot of canoodling (what the Brits call snuggling).

At the keyboard recording an album

Coming home, Rusty and I moved into our new home in Southern California. Today it would be called a *Tiny House*, because it was all of about 500 square feet. It was a cottage behind the house of one of the other pastors on staff. I joined Rusty in his position as Music and Single's Pastor at a church in Southern California. Being a pastor's wife was extremely comfortable for me. I felt that this was what I was born to do. Shepherding and encouraging others seemed natural gifts God had given me. Growing deep relationships with others had always been the lifestyle I loved best. Looking back, I think that little-girl-button of wanting to belong, flourished best when I stayed in one place where I could develop deep and lasting relationships.

The Senior Pastor at our church had given us the freedom to travel one or two Sundays a month, performing concerts nationally and internationally. We created an album during this time that we sold with us when we did concerts.

At that time, we were able to take a remarkable concert tour to Singapore and Malaysia a little over a year into our marriage. The sponsoring church was a mega church there in Singapore. Ten services were held each Sunday, from sunup to sundown, to accommodate all the people. At the end of the 6-week tour, the Senior Pastor asked us to pray about joining his leadership team full time.

This was a dream come true for Rusty, as he had always thrived in other cultures. I was less enthusiastic, as I was completely happy where we were. The thought of living in another culture reminded me of the insecurities I had experienced in Hawaii. I was just starting to feel like I belonged at the church we were at. It was gratifying to see the spiritual growth in those we served. However, within a short period of time, we resigned, packed our suitcases, and moved to Singapore. The year was 1984; we had been married for two years.

Secure at Last

Chapter 9
1984—1985

Made in Singapore

The early morning is hot and heavy with humidity. My body is pregnant and sluggish as I shuffle the short distance from the bedroom to our tiny kitchen. Already, the potent smell of garlic and onion greets me and I try not to gag. My stomach is anything but hungry, but I know if I don't want to start heaving, I need to find some papaya to neutralize the nausea. I groggily rub my eyes as I take a look inside the refrigerator; hoping to get lucky and find a couple slices of papaya left.

Hearing a slight shuffling noise behind me, I turn around, and am totally unprepared for what I see. A creature with pointy ears has his head popped out of the garbage can and his beady little eyes are looking right at me. Our eyes meet and all hell breaks loose. "Ahhhhhh," I scream as my body goes into high gear racing into the bedroom and slamming the door. "Oh my gosh! Oh my gosh! What in the world is that?!" I scream out loud to nobody but myself. Rusty is away on a ministry trip, so I'm all alone to face this animal; this strange little creature that looks like a possum with sharp pointed teeth. The reason I notice his teeth is because of the hissing noise he makes. Yes, a creepy hissing noise.

It takes a few minutes, but I work myself up finally to open the bedroom door and creep back into the other room. As I do, this animal comes running by my feet and into the bedroom as fast as he can. And this time, I get a good look at him. He's massively huge! Well, he's as big as a squirrel, his ears are pointed, and he has a long ropey tail. I've never seen anything like this before, and certainly not in my house!

I run as fast as I can to find my gardener, the Chinese man with one tooth who doesn't understand a word of English. He's the only person I can think of who can help me, so I proceed to scream and yell and make hissing sounds like a maniac, hoping he'll figure out I have a creature in my bedroom. He looks at me blankly and somewhat amused until I stop my antics and succumb to going back to my scary apartment.

There's nothing else to do but wait on the couch for my neighbor Angie to get home. I know that she will fully understand because she's a businesswoman who dresses in a suit every day to go to work downtown. It seems like a very long time before I hear the jingle of Angie's keys next door. Springing into action, I run outside just in time to intercept her before she gets into her apartment. My words tumble out in a jumble, but somehow, she manages to see my plight.

"Ok. You have a king rat in your apartment. I will go to the gardener and ask him to help us. We need to catch the rat and then drown him."

"What? That big creature is a rat?" I ask in disbelief.

"Yes. They are called king rats and can grow as big as squirrels. Let me tell you that they can be very dangerous and mean if threatened."

I go to sleep that night with eyes and ears alert, as the trap sits right in the next room.

The morning light peers into my bedroom the next morning, and I suddenly remember that there could be a hissing creature in my apartment. With heart pounding, I open the door very slowly and peer into the next room. And there it is! As I creep closer it hisses at me, and I notice that it has scooted the trap/cage to reach a nearby blanket. The blanket is in shreds. As I get a little closer, it makes a loud foreboding noise.

Quickly I get changed and run to get Angie and the gardener, wondering what the next step will be. Looking at the rat, Angie says, "Very glad you caught him. He is very angry. You need to come with me while the gardener drowns him." That is just fine with me as I really don't want to be a part of any of this. But then to my utmost surprise she says, "If you watch him die Sherry, your baby will come out with rat ears."

"What?! Are you serious Angie?" I ask with a laugh, thinking that she must be kidding.

She looks at me sternly and assures me matter-of-factly that she has indeed seen this happen to someone before.

Rusty and I first arrived in Singapore in October of 1984. While looking for an apartment to rent, we stayed at the King's Hotel for a week. On one of our first nights there, I had a crazy dream that left me crying real tears as I woke up. I had never had a maternal instinct and wondered why girls would ever want to have children when it was so much work. But, in this dream, I had birthed an ANT; yes, a small, insignificant insect that crawls on the ground kind-of-ant. I absolutely loved this ant with all my heart and tried to nourish and protect it from getting hurt.

Secure at Last

One day a large foot approached and to my horror, it stomped on my ant, squishing it to death. I sobbed so hard that I woke myself up crying. Ok, I realize this was an insanely crazy dream, but I was really heart crushed. And because of it, for the first time I felt a maternal instinct. I could now relate to all the maternal women who wanted to be mothers. I shared my crazy dream with Rusty and then announced, "I really want a baby. How about we get rid of the birth control?" This suited him just fine. At the age of 37, his biological clock was ticking.

About six weeks after arriving in Singapore, I noticed that I had skipped my monthly cycle and wasn't feeling very well. We decided to get a pregnancy test done by one of the doctors in the church. At the beginning of the appointment, I was led to a small room and given a cup to collect my urine sample. Looking around, I realized that there was no toilet in the room, so quizzically I returned to the doctor. "Uh, Doctor Win? I'm not sure if I'm in the right room. I don't see a toilet."

Dr. Win cocked his head sideways and looked at me with his eyebrows raised. *No, is right room*, he said with his thick Chinese accent.

No toilet, I responded. He guided me back to the room. Using his hands, he signified the slant of the floor and then pointed to the drainage hole in the corner. *You go there*, he directed. I politely smiled back at him, as I realized that we were in Old China Town and there was no toilet, just a hole in the corner of a slanted room.

After submitting my sample, we waited a couple days, and received the news that the test was negative. I was surprised and pretty disappointed but accepted the verdict for what it was. However, three weeks later with still another missed cycle and the symptoms growing more intense, we headed to a modern downtown doctor for another test. This time it was positive, and we both rejoiced together that we were going to start a new family.

We had moved into a little apartment about three miles from downtown Singapore. The city was a bustling crowded place. Loud music blared out of crowded shops that lined the streets, and there were restaurants galore. We quickly learned to haggle (barter) and it became a fun game to see how far down we could get the original price. The food in Singapore is simply delicious. In my opinion, no other food in the world compares. Everything is prepared fresh with a plethora of fresh spices and seasoning. There were predominantly two choices of food: East Indian and Singaporean Chinese.

The Singaporean dishes boasted of garlic, onions, and other exotic spices that virtually exploded in your mouth. And if you like heat, the Indian curry was some of the hottest I had ever experienced. They served the curry on a banana leaf on the floor where you sat cross-legged using your hands as a fork. I remember my face sweating, my nose running, and nothing to wipe them with except my shoulder. But wow that was good curry. They label the foods into two categories: *heating* and *cooling*. Heating foods are spicy, and warm you on the inside. Cooling foods are freshly chopped vegetables and fruit to cool your inside.

One of the heating foods, grown primarily in Asia, is called durian. It is affectionately known as *stink fruit* because it literally smells like the combination of a sewer and garlic. If you can handle the odor and get to the poignant taste of actually eating it, a strange phenomenon occurs. It begins to raise your body temperature and can even give you a fever for up to three days. The odor of the fruit exudes from your sweat glands for days. I call it the *Asian birth control*. Singaporeans love it and say that it tastes like cantaloupe after you've eaten it for the third time. They take great pride in the fact that they love it.

When we lived there, thirty-seven years ago, Singapore was a very diverse country. The beautiful downtown area boasted of some of the most modern and beautifully crafted high rises in the world. To this day, the Singaporeans take pride in their country as one of the cleanest and safest in the world. There are laws against anything that would tarnish that reputation, and monetary fines for committing those intolerable acts. If caught chewing gum, you would receive a fine. If caught with illegal drugs or firearms, the death penalty would be implemented. While we were there, an Australian who smuggled drugs into the country was executed. One unlucky American High School student was caned three times for spray-painting graffiti on a wall at school. Caning there is no joke; it causes broken legs and sometimes lifelong injuries. As you might expect it was a safe country with very little crime.

Because Singapore is a very small island, less than 300 square miles, with a population of nearly six million, most people are put on a waiting list for several years for approval to buy a flat (apartment). The terrain consists of high-rise buildings as far as your eye can see. I remember longing to look at an open space of continuous land, but there were only two places like that. One was at the airport, and the other was Sentosa Island, a beautiful, lush garden resort. I would find any opportunity to drive to one of these two spots whenever I started to feel shut in and claustrophobic.

An Indonesian Village

Our roles of ministry at the church were teaching Adult Classes, helping lead worship on Sundays (at all ten services), and singing and preaching for rallies. Rusty taught on weekdays at the Bible College. We also traveled to Malaysia and Indonesia for concerts. One I will never forget was a special Christmas program in Indonesia where we were the guest singers with a massive choir.

It was called *Raja Damai*, translated to the *Peaceful King*. Because of its Christian message, this was an unusual event in a Muslim country. Surprisingly, even a few government officials attended. I'm not sure how the organizers pulled it off, but it was well attended and thrilling to see the gospel message shared with a predominantly Muslim audience.

Secure at Last

During our time in Singapore, I ended up getting parasites. Unfortunately, the effects on my digestion lasted for weeks. I remember one humiliating event during this intestinally explosive sickness. We had double booked two services in different countries. I ended up taking the service in Kuala Lumpur, Malaysia, and Rusty took the other. I was traveling by bus, about 227 miles and four and half hours of driving time.

During the journey, there were potty stops at outhouses along the way. One such outhouse, had doors that rose about 3 feet off the ground. For that reason, I'm not sure why they even had doors? As I got out of the bus, the men in line motioned with their hands for me to go ahead of them to the front of the line. Appalled at the thought of a bunch of strangers watching me go potty, I tried to dissuade them by waving them off. But they insisted. I'm sure they were inwardly smirking at this white lady's dilemma. I knew that if I squatted, I would be visible entertainment for everyone standing there. So, I went in, shut the door, and pretended to do my duty.

As the bus ride continued, I tried to ignore the churning in my unsettled intestines. I comforted myself with the thought that there would be a flush toilet when I reached my destination. But, as fate would have it, the bus was behind schedule, and I ended up arriving to the church late. The service had already started. I walked in discreetly to the front row seat the pastor had saved for me. By the time I sat down, my intestines were gurgling warning signs at me. *You can hold on just a little bit longer,* I tried to console myself.

Just then I heard someone introducing me, so I shuffled up to the platform keeping all my focus on preventing my intestinal tract from exposing itself. The song introduction began playing. It was a duet with Sandy Patti and Lionel Harris called *More Than Wonderful.* Since Rusty wasn't there, I was singing both parts. At the peak of the song, Sandy hits a high ceiling note which was at the very top of my vocal range. Painfully and with sweat on my brow, I hit the note and ended the song. So far, so good. I was just preparing to jet to the nearest bathroom when I heard explosive clapping and the pastor saying, "Oh Mrs. Peavy they want you to do it again." My heart skipped a beat, and the man in charge of playing the tape started it over. I don't know how I made it through the second time, but I know that afterwards, I was in the bathroom for an embarrassingly long time.

We saw many people come to Christ while we were there. Our hearts were filled with gratitude to see what God was doing. What was amazing was to see the countenance change on a Hindu's face who had accepted Christ's love. They literally went from faces that looked like death to faces that shone with Christ's love. Converting from Hinduism to Christianity was a turning from gods who were angry and hated them, to a God who loved them so much He died for them.

Enjoying pregnancy

Rusty worked every weekday at the Bible College, so I spent a lot of time alone with very little connection with people. I didn't have a car, so I mostly sat at home dealing with morning sickness and depression. My heart struggled with homesickness and loneliness much of the time. Here it was again, that little girl button of not belonging, and feeling out of place. I'm sure hormones and culture shock contributed to my sense of loneliness. Hours seemed like days, and days seemed like weeks.

I longed for my family, friends, and the familiar sights and smells of my own culture. It seemed overwhelming, and I begged Rusty to let us go home to have the baby. I concluded that I just wasn't cut out to live overseas, even though my husband was happiest there. This became a source of contention down the road. After we had been there eight months, he finally agreed, and we moved back to our homeland.

Secure at Last

On the way home, we stopped in several countries in Asia. Japan was bursting with their beautiful Cherry Blossom season. It was gorgeous. China was a bustling country with a mix of old and new. Navigating through the streets was a bit tricky. Everywhere I looked there were cars, rickshaws, buses and bicycles, with seemingly no traffic rules in play at all. Everyone made their own lane and maneuvered at their own risk. I'm sure there was some sort of system. But to me, it looked like pure chaos.

One of the provinces we visited was in the southern part of China across from Viet Nam. While there, I didn't see a single Caucasian person. I had never been anywhere like this before, and it felt a little strange to be stared and pointed at wherever we went. It had been a long flight and the time change was catching up with me. Touring one of the city's many street malls, we stopped at one point to rest against a store window. I didn't take much notice, but apparently there were some white mannequins displayed inside the windows we were leaning against. With my eyes closed, I started to relax and drift off until I felt a little tap on my leg. I opened my eyes, and a little boy let out a blood curdling scream. He was looking at me like he had seen a ghost as he ran screaming back to his mommy. Apparently, the little guy had thought I was one of the mannequins that had come to life. We all had quite the belly laugh over that.

Also in that province, we visited some underground church leaders. I will never forget the conversation I had with one remarkably interesting man. He told me that he was the pastor of an underground church, as well as a teacher of Communism in the University. When I questioned how he could fulfill both of those seemingly opposite roles, he answered matter-of-factly, "I ask the students to pick three different religions to compare with Communism. They invariably choose Christianity, which gives me the opportunity to teach the Gospel message." What an amazingly creative way to get the gospel message out in Communist China.

Secure at Last

Chapter 10
1985— 1987

Mama Love

I am extremely emotional as I get off the plane at LAX, Los Angeles International Airport. I want to bend down and kiss the ground, but my fat belly prevents me from doing that. America, my home sweet home! How strange that nobody is taking a second look at me and my white-blond hair. No child is pointing at me. How strange and how wonderful! I am just like everyone else. I love America! Balancing my pregnant body onto the escalator stairs, I am bubbling over with excitement. I wonder who came to pick us up? Will it be Rusty's Mom and Dad or maybe his sister Cherie? It seems like we've been gone forever, and it's only been eight months.

Secure at Last

'SURPRISE!! Welcome home!" I can hear people screaming and look down to see the whole Peavy clan at the bottom of the escalator holding banners and signs saying *Welcome Home Rusty and Sherry!* My heart is exploding with happiness as I fall into the arms of those I know and love well. I am home!

"Look at your shirt! That's hilarious!" Cindy laughs. My shirt says *Made in Singapore* with an arrow pointing down to my pregnant belly. I had it made so nobody would think I was just fat. Of course, all the girls have to pat my belly! And of course, we all talk at the same time.

"What names have you picked out?" Cherie asks.

"Christina Marie. Well, of course her middle name has to be Marie since that's a Peavy tradition, right?" I beam.

"But, how do you know it's a girl?" Lisa inquisitively asks.

I go on to explain that it is a regular practice in Singapore for the doctors to tell you the sex of the baby after a sonogram. This is news to everyone because here in America they haven't quite gotten to that point of proficiency yet. I explain to her that the sonogram showed that we were having a girl. We proceed to Baggage Claim excitedly talking and laughing all at the same time.

After staying a few days with Rusty's wonderful family, we ventured up to our destination, my parent's home in San Jose. With three weeks until the due date, I relished the familiar comforts of home. The baby was due on July 4, 1985. With no insurance or job, somehow, we managed to have my former OB GYN agree to deliver the baby with our Medi-Cal insurance.

Nathan (meaning *gift of God*) Russell Peavy was born right on his due date after a gnarly eight hours of non-medicated labor. To our huge surprise, he was an 8 lb. 6-ounce BOY. We were shocked! After three girl-baby showers, we had a lot of pink girlie clothes to return. But none of that mattered. When I looked into my little boy's eyes for the first time, I experienced a love that I had never felt before. It was as if the whole world had changed!

Rusty and I cried happy tears for this little part of us that was ours to cherish and take care of. When everyone went home that night, I finally got the chance to have my first alone time with my son. I held and caressed him as fireworks for the 4th of July were going off outside in the night sky. This all seemed perfectly appropriate as if the world were cele-brating the birth of my firstborn. It was a special moment where I felt God's presence and it was then that I surrendered him to God and knew that he was born for a special purpose.

Our Made-in-Singapore Baby Nathan

The first couple months of Nathan's life, we continued to live with my parents while looking for an Associate Pastor's position. I was so thankful for Mom's assistance as Nathan was up every night crying with a colicky stomach. After interviewing with a church in the Sacramento area, we were hired as music and singles' pastors. Rusty and I were thrilled to move our little family the 120 miles and set up our new household in Sacramento County.

My days were filled with loving and taking care of our baby boy. I also came alongside Rusty as the piano player for the church and choir, as well as putting together activities for the Singles Group. We developed many wonderful friendships during our three years there. I felt extremely fulfilled in raising our son and serving the people of the church.

Secure at Last

A couple of years later, we reached out to another Assembly of God church in the area and were hired for the same position. Whether good or bad, when we left the first church, quite a few people followed us to the new church; not because we encouraged it, but because of the close friendships we had developed.

I came into this new church position a bit uneasy. During the interview with the new Senior Pastor, I had a strong check in my spirit that something wasn't quite right. I talked to Rusty about it, but he didn't share the same feeling. I had learned to listen to these strong inner urgings, as usually there was a good reason for them. When our spirit is united with God's Spirit, He can speak to us through deep intuitions.

The transition into our new role was easy since we were essentially doing the same job. We were able to stay in our home and quickly loved the new congregation we were privileged to serve. Rusty was happy to have the opportunity to preach more often, something that he had been desiring to do for some time. I started a young moms' Bible Study and saw God work in the lives of many young women.

By now, I was eight months pregnant again, and we were excited to welcome our new baby into this world. We were secretly hoping for a girl since we wanted one of each. However, we didn't want to ask about the gender because of the mistake that happened in Singapore. I was unusually large. From the time I was seven months pregnant, people repeatedly asked if the baby was due soon.

By the time I was full term, I couldn't judge my belly size and it would periodically bump into people and objects. At one point I thought about putting a red flag on the end of it. One Sunday morning, the pastor was closing the service and asked me to play the piano softly while he gave the altar call. I tiptoed to the platform as quietly as I could, but as soon as I sat down my belly hit the keys with a loud bang. This broke the quiet serene atmosphere, and the pastor wasn't very happy about it. It was October 19, and I was ten days overdue and ready to get the baby out.

Secure at Last

That evening in desperation, I went to a pharmacy to buy some castor oil because I had heard that it could induce labor. The store had just closed, and all the doors were locked. I know this because I tried them all. However, I could see the workers still bustling about the store, so I banged on the door as loud as I could. For a while they ignored me. But when I didn't stop, someone finally opened the door. Maybe they saw the way my head was spinning around and about to fly off my head! I bought the castor oil, took it home, and drank as much as I could stomach. To my dismay, all it did at first was cause me a lot of trips to the bathroom. I went to sleep resigned to be eternally pregnant.

At 2:00 the next morning, my water broke, and I immediately went into intense labor. By the time I got to the hospital and asked for drugs, (this time I didn't want to be a hero) they wouldn't give me any because I was already dilated to seven cm. Our baby girl was born two hours later, on October 20 and weighed a whopping ten pounds. We cried tears of joy to welcome, not only another child into our family, but the girl that we had been hoping for. In our minds, our family was complete; a boy and a girl, and we were ecstatic! We named her Melissa Marie.

Our son Nathan was two at the time. He was opinionated and knew exactly what he liked and what he didn't and wasn't afraid to tell us. Melissa was quite the opposite. She loved everything and everybody and wasn't particular about anything. We marveled at how these two little humans from the same gene pools could be so different. They each brought so much joy into our world in their own distinct ways. I wouldn't trade them then or now for anyone else in the world. I had never felt so

Melissa and Nathan

fulfilled as I did then; two beautiful children to love, and a new congregation full of rich friendships. Little did I know that a month later, my world was going to change. Again!

Chapter 11
1987—1992

Black Friday

Pulling up to a stop, I turn my right blinker on at the light. "Wow, Black Friday traffic gets worse every year. I wouldn't step a foot into a mall right now," I say to my brother Steve and parents in the back seat. "You guys I think we're barely going to make it in time to see the movie, so I'll drop you all off at the entrance and find a parking space. Could you take Nathan in with you too?"

'Sure!" My parents both chime in.

'What the heck is this guy doing?" From out of the line of oncoming traffic, a car darts out and starts racing toward us.

"Surely, he sees us. What is he doing? He's coming straight for us!" My heart pounds, and then a loud crashing sound!

A bit dazed, I assess the situation. Nathan is untouched in his car seat next to me. I turn around and see that my mom, dad, and brother all seem to be fine. I feel fine too. So, I jump out and see that the front of my car is completely totaled. Pumping with adrenaline and madder than a hornet, I race to the other car and start screaming at the driver, "What the heck were you doing you jerk? Get out of the car!"

People are getting out of their cars and running up to our car. They seem concerned about me.

"Ma'am you need to sit down."

But all I can think about is yelling at the perpetrator. As they pull me back to my car and put me back in the driver's seat, I am confused as to why they are so concerned about me. Before I know it, there is a light shining in my eyes and a police officer asking me a myriad of questions about who I am and where I live.

"Why does he keep asking me how old I am? This is getting annoying. Why isn't he concerned with the driver who hit me?"

The longer he talks, the more annoyed and agitated I get. I try to get out of the car, but the police officer holds me down, and I hear him say, "Ma'am please don't move. Try to stay still. You've been injured." There are a lot of people talking, and suddenly I'm aware of a major headache. I hear the police officer call for an ambulance, and notice blood is coming down my face into my eyes.

As I lay in the MRI machine at the hospital, I thought of the day before. It had been one of the best Thanksgiving Days I'd ever had. Our house had been bustling with family and friends visiting from out of town. It was so fun to see everyone playing with Nathan and holding baby Melissa. Good food, good family, and good fun was had by all.

Now, here I lay with a crazy load of questions swirling in my head. *Was everybody else in the car ok? Oh God, help Nathan to be ok! I wonder what happened to me because my head hurts really bad. Why did that guy drive straight into us? We were right out in the open. What was he thinking?*

After several X-rays, I received the grave news that I might have broken my neck and that if I moved wrong, it could paralyze me. They put me in a halo, and I waited to have more X-rays done. After the second set of scans, I was given the good news that my neck wasn't broken. Strangely enough, the X-ray in doubt had shown a shadow from a tooth that apparently looked like a fractured neck. The truth was that my jaws, not my neck, had actually been fractured. That would explain the intense headache that had started right after the accident.

The doctors made the decision to hold off on any surgery or wiring of my jaw because I was so thin. They were concerned that the weight loss would negatively affect my health. I returned home with an intense pain that radiated from my jaw to the top of my head and down my neck and shoulders. Talking, eating, laughing, or any other use of my jaw was extremely limited because of the pain. Hmmm…another issue with talking. Was God trying to tell me something?

To say that my life abruptly and profusely changed from this event is an understatement. I had constant 24-hour pain that never let up, and it worsened by any movement of my jaw. I had to stop doing everything I loved; going to church, working, teaching, or any other activity that included talking. I couldn't chew and ate only foods that could be pureed to a baby food consistency.

I remember being so tired of milkshakes and sweetened foods like yogurt, that I experimented with grinding a steak up in a food processor. I quickly realized that one cannot underestimate the importance of consistency and texture. Drinking steak quickly takes your appetite away.

During the first few months, I rapidly lost weight and looked very haggard and drawn. It's sad that most people have no pity for people who are too thin. When I would tell my friends that I wished I could gain weight, they'd just look at me with that look that says "Really? Please."

Until this accident, I had never realized how chronic pain wears on you. It can take an easy-going person and turn them into Godzilla. I struggled to keep my attitude kind and loving with my kids. But you moms know that having toddlers can push you to the brink of sanity at times. There were a few times that I remember just reaching my limit. I would take both kids and put them in a safe place, walk out to my driveway and just run around my parked car several times. I didn't go anywhere, just ran and ran. My neighbors didn't say a word.

If you've never had chronic pain, it's hard to understand how it can wear on your last nerve and drive you to the brink of despair. I enrolled Nathan in preschool and Melissa at a friend's home daycare so that I could get therapy and chiropractic treatments three times a week. Even then, I lived in constant pain for four years.

Two years after the accident, Rusty came home from work and announced, "You're never going to believe what happened to me today. I got fired. Pastor told me to pack up and leave immediately." At first, I thought he had to be joking, but he assured me that it was all true.

"Why? What on earth happened?" I asked in a state of shock.

Rusty looked like a deer in the headlights. He explained, "Well, the other Associate Pastor and I confronted Pastor with our suspicions that he was having an affair with a choir member. We also showed him the proof we had that he was embezzling thousands of dollars from the church account. He completely denied it and fired us right there on the spot. In fact, he told us that we were never again to have contact with any of the people in church; he used the verse that talks about excommunicating the black sheep from the church. Can you believe it?" The next few hours, we both reeled from the shock and gravity of this decision. What were we going to do now with our lives? Our livelihoods? Our friends?

A few days later, we were told that on the following Sunday morning the pastor had gotten up and told the congregation that we were being excommunicated because we had done something terribly wrong. He never explained what it was, but instead issued a warning that nobody was to have any contact with us because we were considered black sheep.

Bewildered and reeling from the gravity of our situation, I thought about my upcoming jaw surgery the following Monday. Who would help us with the meals, housecleaning and all the other things that our church family did for each other during hard times? I was so extremely upset at the inequity of the situation. The pastor seemed to be getting a free pass for his sins by blaming us. The anger boiled deep inside me, and I found myself hating this man; an emotion I had not felt in a long time.

Even with the pastor's warning, several people dropped off meals after my surgery. It was surreal. They would ring our doorbell and then run to their car without saying a word to us. I felt so sad for our friends who knew that we were in need, but also felt compelled to obey the pastor. It was very awkward for everyone involved. This was my third jaw surgery since the accident and again it was unsuccessful in easing the pain. After the surgeries, countless therapy, chiropractic treatments, pain medicine, and splint devices, I had to resign myself to the idea that I might have this horrible headache and neck pain for the rest of my life.

We were jobless and not sure what to do. Rusty began trying to talk me out of my decision to never live overseas again. He knew that I had come back from Singapore determined to never live in another culture again. But his desire to go was strong. "You know, we could just go for a one-year assignment and see how that goes," he prodded. This questioning went on for a few months. When I reluctantly agreed to a year, he began to talk about a two or three-year assignment. After the continued prodding, 1 finally agreed. I was tired of fighting it, and felt I had no choice.

As a little girl I had been taught that the man was the leader of the house, and the wife was to submit to his authority. I had observed women who had kept their husbands from doing things they desperately wanted to do. It seemed to always backfire into bitterness, which affected their marriage for years. I certainly didn't want this to happen to us, so I conceded to going even though I wasn't comfortable with it.

Since that time in my life, I have learned that the scripture teaches that both women and men are to submit to one another in love at various times. Ephesians 5:21 NIV says, *Submit* to one another *out of reverence for Christ*. (My emphasis) In other words, because of our love for Christ, husbands and wives should each submit to one another. Jesus said that the two most important commandments are to love God with all our heart, and to treat others the way we want to be treated. This is not gender specific.

After I conceded to going overseas again, we started the process of applying with the missionary board of our denomination. It was quite a detailed process with references, personality and gifting tests, language acquisition assessment, as well as detailed essay questions about your past and present experiences. After passing the first phase, we were then flown to the headquarters in Springfield, Missouri, and interviewed personally by the board. It was there that we almost didn't make the cut, due to our request to go for a short-term assignment of three years.

At that time, most of the missionaries sent overseas by our denomination went with the commitment to serve for a lifetime. This is what the board wanted to hear from us. The men wanted to know why we couldn't make a commitment for life to missions. At one point, a member of the board intervened on our behalf by reminding the seasoned group of ministers that Rusty and I were from a different generation, the Baby Boomers, and were not comfortable taking jobs for a lifetime. He suggested to the group that they needed to look at changing their expectations for this new Boomer generation. It was because of this man that we were given the go ahead.

Soon afterward, we gathered up our little family, and flew to a six-week missionary training course in another state. About 80 other new missionary folks joined us. We all lived on the campus at a local Bible College, where we slept in the dorms and ate in the cafeteria. Each day we attended specialized classes from morning until night. We were taught how to live in another culture, modes of sharing the gospel, target ministry groups, and so much more. The kids attended a day camp where they had a lot of fun field trips and activities. They had their own church services as well.

Almost all the missionaries knew where they were going except Rusty and me. Initially we were sure that God would speak to us and that we would know before the end of the six weeks. However, when the final week arrived and we still had no idea where we were going, we had to come up with a plan. "Maybe we should fast and pray," I suggested. "We could use the chapel every night after the session is over. We need to get serious and hear from God. What do you think?" Out of desperation, I was becoming bolder.

Rusty agreed. "Yeah, and I don't think we should tell each other what we hear God saying until the end of the week. That way we won't influence each other." That sounded perfect. Every night after the last group session, we'd get the kids to sleep and then go into the chapel to pray and listen, journaling whatever we heard.

At the end of the week, we spent the morning comparing notes from our journals. Rusty couldn't get these words out of his head, "I can't get anybody to go." As for me, God spoke to me in a familiar way, through a vision. It was a recurring vision of myself, sitting on a chair in front of a hut. Around me in a semi-circle sat black-skinned ladies, sitting cross-legged on a large mat. I was teaching them from a Bible on my lap. With only these two clues, Rusty and I still didn't know what country this description fit.

The news spread amongst the leaders that we were still praying about where we were going. On one of the last days, three different Area Directors sat down with us separately and shared their country's needs. I remember when the South African Director shared about the black-skinned people in Cape Town, I thought maybe that's what I had seen in my vision.

However, we were stunned when the South Pacific Director shared these exact words with us— "I can't get anybody to go there." He was talking about the island nation of Fiji. Rusty blurted out that he had heard these same words in his head. I wasn't convinced because in my experience, South Pacific Islanders were brown skinned. The Director went on to tell us that the people in Fiji had migrated from Africa and looked like the black-skinned women in my vision. Apart from my apprehension about living overseas again, I started to get excited. It was apparent that God had shown up. If He wanted to use us there, I would surrender and go. We both said a resounding "yes" to go to Fiji.

Prayer and commissioning to Fiji

The next steps were to plan a budget for our three-year term and raise our financial support. We were to go to churches in our district and hold services asking for pledges of monthly support. This meant every weekend and sometimes midweek, Rusty, the kids, and I traveled to various cities and shared about the needs in Fiji. Sometimes we even dressed in the native garb: a sarong, called a *sulu*, that wraps around your waist or shoulders.

During that time, there happened to be a surge of missionaries planning to go overseas. As a result, it was 2 1/2 years before we were able to move to Fiji. I tried to go with Rusty on the weekends, but many times the pain and headaches constrained me. I was still going to the chiropractor and physical therapy three times a week, wearing a mouth splint, as well as limiting my talking, singing, and chewing. But still, the pain persisted. It was all I could do to take care of the kids and the house. I tried not to dwell on the fears of how my limitations would affect me overseas. We continued to pray for a miracle of healing.

By this time, the pastor who had fired us at the church had long since been exposed and fired for his wrong doings. I remember that I wanted to get rid of my hateful feelings towards him but didn't know how. About three months after we were fired, Rusty and I were called and asked to make an appointment with the Area Pastor who oversaw all the pastors in our region. I was dreading this meeting because I didn't want this Pastor to know all the hatred and anger I held inside.

During the meeting, the Area Pastor asked us to voice our feelings about what we had gone through with him. I disguised my hate with words like *hurt* and *wounded*. The words *hate* and *anger* seemed too harsh for a ministry wife to be feeling. However, I wasn't fooling this man.

He looked right at me and asked, "Do you want to forgive this man and be free from your hatred?" He explained that anger and unforgiveness toward another only hurt us. It ties us to them, and we carry them on our shoulders with emotions that continue to cripple us. Forgiving them doesn't mean they weren't wrong in what they did, it just keeps them from hurting us again by the anger held inside. I tried not to look astonished at the fact that he could see right through me. I gulped and said quite honestly that I really wanted to forgive him but didn't know how.

He asked if I would be willing to do an exercise with him. When I agreed, he put a chair in front of me and asked me to envision the pastor who had hurt me sitting in that chair. He said he wanted me to tell the man all the things he had done that had wounded me. He gave me permission to call him every name in the book and even yell and scream if I wanted to. I did just that. I yelled and screamed and told him how the horrible things he had done had screwed up my life. At the end of my rant, he said, "Ok, now I want you to say, 'I forgive you Pastor (his name) as if you never did anything to me.'"

After I completed this exercise, he continued. "Now you're not going to *feel* like you have forgiven him. But your *feelings* aren't what's important right now. It's your *choice* that's important. Every time you begin to play the offenses over in your mind, stop and say the words out loud, 'I forgive you, Pastor (his name). It's as if you never did anything to me.' When you hear other people speaking negatively about this person, reiterate to them that you have chosen to forgive him and don't want to talk about him." He also told me that I needed to pray for him every day.

He reminded me again that my feelings of forgiveness may not come for a long time and that forgiving the pastor didn't mean what he did was right, nor did it absolve him of his wrongdoing. It just freed me, so that I no longer carried it, and didn't have to suffer down the road.

Through all this, I learned that unforgiveness and anger can cause a wide range of emotional and physical harm. Studies have revealed that even cancer can stem from unresolved negative feelings.

I left there with a load of wisdom that I needed to put into practice. I was given that opportunity time and time again, whether it was affirming my forgiveness to others who talked about him, or my own thoughts of character assassination. I would literally get on my knees and pray aloud for him and his family. At first there were no feelings of forgiveness at all. It was just words. But, little by little in the weeks and months to come, I started seeing my prayers become more genuine. And instead of hating him, I started to feel pity and sorrow for him.

It took a few months, but I can honestly say that I was freed from the weight of the anger and hatred. I felt a new freedom and lightness in my step. This has become a valuable tool and one I have learned to use when wronged. I assure you that there is nothing worth hating over. It only robs you of joy and health. It is your choice, and one that you and you alone can make. If you are struggling with someone who has wronged you, I urge you to take these steps toward forgiveness. I am living proof that you can be set free, and free for life.

Secure at Last

Chapter 12
1992—1998

Bula Vinaka! Fiji, Here We Come!

Lying on the couch, I am crushed with the overwhelming reality that we are flying to our new *home* overseas in two weeks to take on a whole new life. *Oh, dear God, tonight I couldn't even go with Rusty to a service down the street because of this gripping pain in my neck and shoulders. How am I going to move to a foreign land and leave the team of doctors here? If three surgeries and weekly therapy appointments haven't helped, what's going to happen when I'm living in a third-world country with no help at all?*

And just then I hear Him; a thought downloaded as clear as a bell. *Sherry, can you trust me for this moment? Just this very moment. Not for next month, next week, tomorrow, or even in an hour. But can you trust me for this very second? And then the next. And then the next...*

I sincerely mull this over in my mind. It's so hard to think about the future. It's scary and unknown. But can I trust God right now at this very present moment that I am living? And with a faith not my own, I respond out loud with rugged and bare honesty, "Yes, I can trust You for this very second Father. And I'll try to trust You for the next one, and then the next."

I found myself taking little baby steps for the next few hours and days. When I would get scared and flustered, I would again turn my focus and attention on the trustworthiness of Jesus for that very moment.

After three long years, we had finally finished raising our financial support and were packing all our goods into a shipping container. It was mind boggling. Each box had to have an itemized list of its contents, including quantity and monetary value, in case of damage or loss. We had hundreds of boxes. Thank the Lord for my mom and amazing girlfriends, Barb, Joy, Julie, and more. They helped me sort and pack, sell and give away, cook and clean, take care of the kids, and stay sane.

Two weeks later, after tearful goodbyes, we landed in Hawaii for a week-long conference with other Asia/Pacific missionaries. The schedule was very loose, so it left us with a lot of time to meet and get to know everyone. The kids were four and six at the time. We all enjoyed going to the beach and hanging out with these new friends.

When the week was almost over, I realized that something was drastically different. The constant pain that I had lived with for the last 3-4 years was lessening day by day. This was a major surprise, as I hadn't been pain-free for even a moment in the previous three years. And when we arrived in Fiji, the pain was completely and totally GONE! A total miracle! What the chiropractor, therapists, splints, surgeries couldn't do in three years, God had done in three weeks! And there is no other explanation but GOD. I have never had that TMJ headache pain since. NEVER! Words could not express my gratitude to God for this healing just before the dawn of the crazy busiest time of life that awaited me ahead.

Secure at Last

After a seven-hour flight from Hawaii, and crossing over the International Dateline, our family landed at the Fiji International Airport in Nadi. We had no idea what to expect. Walking through the open-air airport, I felt my hair sticking to my neck from the heat and humidity. "Hey, friend, Bula Vinaka. Taxi? You need taxi driver? Here, over here." A bunch of noisy taxicab drivers surrounded us clambering for our attention.

Amidst the heat and our exhaustion, we chose an East Indian man who crammed us all into his small car with our luggage. Off we went for the three-hour journey to our new home. Suva is the Capital of Fiji and the place we were going to be living. Much of the journey was on a two-lane road following the coastline. It reminded me a lot of Hawaii, except that the lush vegetation was raw and mostly untouched. Much different from the manicured beauty of Hawaii. If a storm blew a palm tree half over, it usually just stayed that way for the rest of its life. The brush was dense, and the branches twisted and intertwined in their own unintentional pattern.

The Peavy family arrives in Fiji

With Hindi music blaring from the radio, the driver gave us an earful about the state of the government in Fiji. Of course, we got his East Indian take on it. Eventually we gained a broader understanding of Fijian history. About 100 years prior, East Indians were brought to Fiji as indentured laborers on the sugarcane plantations. And now, roughly half the population is East Indian. The country was a British Colony from 1874–1970. When they gained their independence in 1970, they continued to follow the Crown's political system of having a King and Queen as well as a Prime Minister. While we were there from 1992-1998, the King and

Prime Minister were Indigenous Fijians. The taxicab driver aired his frustration in his thick Hindi accent, "Fijian buggas no like when one Indian man get elected. They make trouble in the streets and fight with us till they kick the Indian guy out and put in one of their guys. They say we not Fijian, but I was born in dis place." He ranted with his hands waving about. By birth he was a Fijian citizen.

As we drove to Suva, I realized that driving was going to be a real adventure here. The steering wheel was on the right side of the car, with cars driving on the left side of the road. It seemed the taxi driver put his blinker on often, and for many different reasons. A left signal could be that he was turning left. Or it could mean he was turning right. Or possibly he was going to stop, so the car behind him could pass around. I sat rigid, eyes glued to the road as he passed vehicles on blind curves, all while ranting and throwing his hands up and down.

God, you haven't brought us all the way here to let a car accident take us out, I whispered under my breath. Somehow, we reached our destination safely.

When we first arrived at our new home in Suva, there was a lot to take in. The house and surrounding neighborhood were a pleasant surprise. It was a large, old house with beautiful, lush land surrounding it. I loved that it was on a hill with a large front porch overlooking the ocean about five miles away. I envisioned serving tea to people out on the veranda while watching the children play. I chuckle as I write this early assumption that I would be doing anything leisurely. I had no idea how busy my life was about to become. Thankfully I had no headaches or pain, so I would be up for the tasks ahead.

We enrolled the kids in The International School, a British School with a great mix of students from around the world. About half the kids were local Fijians and half from other countries, especially New Zealand and Australia. It did my heart good to see that Nathan and Melissa would not be ostracized because of their race and color like I had experienced as a child.

The kids made friends quickly and our home and yard became the *hood* for the neighbor kids to hang out. Having a large trampoline in the front yard was a plus. Soon, I was listening to my

Our home in Fiji

children talk with Aussie accents, and from time to time would have to ask them to explain what they had said. Like the day Melissa couldn't understand why everyone was so shocked when she said that she had a blue and a pink rubber. We all laughed when she explained that a rubber was an eraser.

Early on, our kids became best friends with the two neighbor kids two houses down. Our families shared the same ages; all the way from the mom and dad, Rhada and Liz, to the kids, Probesh and Rhea. I loved their kids as if they were my own. We started a kids' club for our neighborhood children. They learned about Jesus and how much He loved them. We explained that He had died for them so that He could take the penalty for their sin and have a relationship with them. One day Rhea's heart was stirred, and she ventured upstairs to my room to talk about it.

She told me she wanted to accept Jesus as her Savior and Lord. The family was Hindu, and I didn't want to do anything that would upset her parents. Respect for elders is important in their culture. So, I called her mom and relayed to her what Rhea wanted to do, "Hey Liz, um, you know the Kid's Club that we have at our house? Well. you know we tell the kids about the Bible, and what it says to do. Today we talked about Jesus being the way to God, and Rhea asked if she could start praying to Jesus. I just wanted to make sure that you were aware of that."

Her answer surprised me. She laughingly said, "Well. Yes. of course. That's fine. Jesus is one of our good teachers too. I've noticed that Rhea seems to be more obedient since she's been going to the Kid's Club. She can just add Jesus to the list of all our other gods that we pray to."

Fast forward to several years after we left Fiji, Rhea grew up to be a gorgeous young woman who went through a battle with cancer when she was 16 years old. She told us that it was her faith that got her through the hard times. As I write this, her mom Liz, has also converted from Hinduism and given her heart to Jesus. She and Rhea are both strong Christian women.

Never underestimate the importance of a child accepting Christ. Statistics say that 80% of people who come to Christ do so before they are 18 years old. Children have what Jesus called *childlike faith*. They haven't been jaded by world experiences and haven't built up walls to keep Him out. Their hearts are like sponges that soak up spiritual things easily and quite naturally. It's sad that Children's Ministry is often the least-funded ministry in church. Since this is the age when most people give their lives to Christ, don't we need to wake up and give that ministry a much higher priority?

Fijian village

I quickly realized that grocery shopping was going to be nearly a full-day event. Come with me on a weekly grocery shopping trip. First, there are four different places to buy what we need for the week. Our first stop is at the outdoor market in downtown Suva, with many food stalls and vendors. You'll smell various potent farm odors and a mixture of dirt and sweet rotting fruit. You'll hear me haggling with the vendors. Just when you think they have said *no* to my offer, they will start bagging it up and giving it to me. It's a game we play to make us each feel we got a fair deal.

Next, we'll go to the butcher market for our meat. These aromas might hit your gag reflex. It smells of flesh and blood. Portions of cows and pigs and whole chickens hang from hooks swarming with flies. Again, the haggling until we reach a deal. The next two stops are on our way home. The bakery is bustling with patrons because Fijians buy their bread fresh daily. The aroma of hot bread will tantalize your taste buds, making you instantly long for a bite. You'll probably be amazed at the many types of breads: with cheese, custards, jams, and other assorted yummy treats.

The last stop we'll make is at Super Fresh Market. This is the store that most resembles our grocery stores in the States. Although, instead of 30 different kinds of cereals, you'll find three. This is where we will buy canned and prepackaged goods. You'll notice that I stop often to read labels because most things are from Australia or New Zealand. The labels may be different from the States. For example, their tomato sauce is literally ketchup. I learned this after putting it in spaghetti sauce, which didn't turn out very well. You'll also notice that I'm buying things our grandmas used to. Because the selection is quite limited, I've learned how to make almost everything from scratch: homemade granola, flour tortillas, chocolate chips, and many more of our American products.

Toward the end of our first year in Fiji, the British Broadcasting Company (BBC) brought in the first television station. It was on from 5:00 P.M.–10:00 P.M. At first most of the programs were British. We watched whatever they aired, even Mr. Bean. Ugh. Can't say I was a fan. Being big fish in a small pond helped Nathan and Melissa to be chosen for a commercial with Roops Big Bear Furniture Store. I'll never forget how excited we were to crowd around the TV and see their little faces.

For a while, I had a puppet program on TV that told children stories about Jesus. We called it *Sherry and the Little Lambs,* and it aired about the time the kids got home from school.

Although there were benefits to having television, there were significant downsides as well. Islanders became aware of the material things that people had in other countries. Shows such as *Dallas* and *Dynasty*, painted a picture of wealth and opulence. Consequently, most Fijians thought that every American was rich. They believed that we all lived in mansions, drove high end cars, and dressed in designer clothes with diamonds. Because of this, crime escalated a hundred percent in that first year, most being theft. Crazy, the influence our media has had on other cultures around the world. And most of it negative.

Before television, Fijians equated wealth with having great relationships and a lot of family. There's a saying in the Fijian language: *Kere Kere*. This means, "What I have is yours and what you have is mine." In other words, we all share. If I have six dresses and you only have one, you can *Kere Kere* me for a dress and I will share some of mine with you. It's a beautiful village concept of taking care of one another.

When television shows like *Dallas* began airing on Fijian TV, the beautiful *Kere Kere* sharing system morphed into "What's yours is mine and I'll take it." Our neighborhood was especially targeted because of the comparatively nicer homes there. Our own little family had quite a few break-ins. In one, they even took my clothes and shoes. It happened so frequently that we almost became accustomed to them, and eventually were unafraid to confront them in the act. I'll share just a few of those with you.

The first time we were robbed, Rusty and I were at our Bible College Graduation Ceremony which was held at the church down the street. My dear friend Annie was watching the kids for us. In the middle of the ceremony, I received a message that there was an emergency at the house and Annie was trying to reach me. I quickly left and went home to find her quite shaken up.

Apparently, while she was putting the kids to sleep, she saw a man walking down the hallway. She laid out the story in anxious detail. "Cheree (the way she pronounced my name), I saw this bugga roaming down the hallway, but he didn't see us cuz the light was off. I didn't want to scare the kids, you know, so I started talking really loudly. I was yelling their bedtime prayer so the guy would hear me and run off. I waited until the kids were asleep and I couldn't hear him anymore, and then I went downstairs and called the church. Hey, you're lucky I was here, man. I would never let anything happen to these two precious little kids." My friend Annie was a tough Fijian woman, and I didn't doubt she would have fought tooth and nail if the kids had been threatened. What she did worked, and the thief ended up leaving without taking anything. After that scary evening, we put bars on our windows as well and installed an alarm system.

Another time, I was home by myself in the evening. It was October 31, America's Halloween, which is ironically also the Hindu Diwali Day, Festival of Lights. The kids were playing at the neighbor's house and Rusty was at an outdoor crusade. I was supposed to have gone with him but kept having a God-premonition that something was not right, and I was supposed to stay home and pray. Not that this happened to me every day. It was quite a strong feeling.

God directed me to a passage of scripture in Psalm 142: 5–6 NIV, *I cry to you, O Lord: I say You are my refuge. Listen to my cry for I am in desperate need: rescue me from those who pursue me.* I had no idea why I was supposed to read that scripture, but I prayed it fervently over and over. I was sitting at my desk looking out the window of the second floor of our house. While praying, I heard something behind me and turned to see what it was. Lo and behold, it

Me at 'the desk'

was a large Fijian man! And he was walking slowly towards me. At first, I wasn't too alarmed, thinking that it might be one of our students who had tried knocking at the door. Then I saw the look in his eyes as he approached me. I knew he was not a friendly visitor.

I stood up and did something totally uncharacteristic of me. Most likely it was because I had just watched a video on self-defense that showed what to do when frightened by a wild animal, such as a mountain lion. First, it had said to get angry instead of scared. Think about what your kids would do if they suddenly didn't have a mother and use that anger to get as big and loud as you can. I figured if it worked for mountain lions, it might work for human enemies as well.

With a strange boldness, I started running at him. His eyes widened and he looked like he had seen a ghost. I tried to jump on him as he ran down the hallway, down the stairs, and out the side door. Just before I slammed the door I screamed, "And don't you come back!" What? Really? Where did that come from?

Going back into the house, I was shocked to see piles of our things next to the door. Apparently, he had been there for a while and was stockpiling the various items he was going to take with him. The shock of what had just happened hit me right after I slammed the door. My heart started pounding and my body shaking. There is no doubt in my mind that God empowered me with boldness and strength during the scripture reading and prayer beforehand. Had I not been filled with His presence at that time, I'm sure I would have responded quite differently.

Another night, I was startled to see something moving down at the end of the hallway in my bedroom. As I walked slowly toward it, I could see that it was a long pole that someone was poking through the window bars in our bedroom upstairs. The pole was going up and down, and as I walked closer to it, I could see that it was trying to loop my purse laying on the bed. *Not again!* I thought as I ran up to the window. The perpetrator dropped the pole and scurried away from the house.

I want to emphasize here that most Fijians are not criminals and are just the opposite of this. They are loving and generous. These stories were about rare individuals who had greedy hearts. This kind of behavior can be found anywhere and in any culture. During most of our time in Fiji we encountered the love and generosity of the people. Fiji is known as *the friendliest place on earth*, and I whole-heartedly concur. They are a happy, carefree people that put relationships first. I went there to teach, but they taught me every bit as much. They really do know how to live in the moment, putting people before material things; something that Americans could most definitely learn from.

One such example of this was when Hurricane Katrina plummeted right through Suva where we lived. We were warned that the eye of the hurricane was going to come through sometime around midnight. Our neighbor Liz called and told us to open the windows on both sides of our house. She explained that the force of the winds would burst all the glass windows, and this could relieve some of the wind pressure.

Sure enough, around midnight, the gusty winds calmed down and it became eerily quiet for a while. The eye of the hurricane was directly over us, and all became still. About 15 minutes later, a deafening roar like a train, screamed through the house. It grew and grew in intensity until the roar was so loud, we couldn't hear each other. For a few hours it blew with such intensity that we could see palm trees and big pieces of board and other debris flying horizontally through the air.

The deafening, screaming, forceful wind was wreaking havoc on our house. The tiles of our roof were being sucked up and torn from the ceiling with rain pouring inside the house in sheets. We bunkered up at the top of the house for the remainder of the night. The next morning when we ventured downstairs, we saw our first floor truly devastated. Much of the ceiling had been damaged and sucked away, and our whole bottom floor living area was covered with thick red mud and water, like a dirty paste. For the next week, there was no running water or electricity. Suva had sustained massive damage.

I learned from experience that living without electricity is one thing. But living without water is another. We couldn't clean the muddy house, let alone ourselves. There was no water for drinking or making food. And then there's the bathroom issue. There was no other place to go but to the hotels and restaurants downtown that were powered by generators. We had to time each of our potty needs together, so we'd only have to make two trips downtown a day.

The Fijians responded to this devastation with so much grace. We were utterly shocked at how they accepted their plight without complaining. Many had lost their houses, their crops, their animals and more, and yet they were literally responding with a no-big-deal attitude. "We are so grateful that our lives were spared," they'd say, and "Hey, it's no big deal; we'll just live with Uncle Joe while we build our houses back and plant more crops."

We watched the islanders rally together to help their family and neighbors get back on their feet. I believe that if this had happened to Americans, they would have considered themselves victims for many years or maybe for the rest of their lives. It might even take years of counseling to completely recover. The beauty of the island way is, "It takes a village" and "People are more important than things." When the rubber hit the road, they showed us what they were made of.

American life is so dictated by our things: our nice homes, cars, the latest technology. Our lives have become complicated as the more stuff we have, the more stuff we want. And the more we get, the more we must work to maintain these things. In the villages in Fiji, most people live in tiny bungalows. Their furniture consists of mats and possibly a makeshift stove and refrigerator. Housework consists of shaking the mats outside and sweeping the floor. The people are not bound to their things, so they are free to enjoy their family and friends. If you were to visit a village, the first thing you would notice is the belly laughs you would hear all around you. Fijians truly know how to enjoy each day to the fullest.

Besides people being more important than things, another Fijian concept is that people are more important than time. For example, if I was running late to a doctor's appointment and saw a person I knew on the way, it would be very impolite to hurry away. That person was more important than the time of the meeting. So, I would stay and chat for as long as they wanted to talk. Obviously, appointment times almost always run late there. However, it's not important to them *when* the meeting occurs; it's only important that it occurs.

I had always been the kind of person that carried a Day-Timer with me. I took great satisfaction in checking off the to-do list as a task was done. This did not work in the Fijian culture. There were many days when students would just stop in unannounced. I'd see people coming up our driveway and know that I needed to throw my plans out the window. My tasks were not as important as having a good *talk-story* with real people. I learned that some of the most important ministry happened right there in the unplanned visits; something else that my Fijian friends taught me.

Students stop by

Secure at Last

Chapter 13
1992—1998

Culture and Ministry

Coming into the kitchen I see Kalera, our housekeeper at the sink doing dishes with her back towards me. I start chatting away like we normally do in the mornings. But when she doesn't turn around and chime in, I figure something must be wrong. "Kalera are you sick? Are you ok? Hey, what's going on?" I ask her, coming around so I can see her eye-to-eye.

It's then that I can see the bruises and cuts all over her face. "Oh no, Kalera. What on earth happened to you, Sweetheart? Is your baby ok? Did anything happen to your baby?" I cry out. Kalera and her husband Sai have been trying to have a baby for 6 years now with several miscarriages along the way. Her body is now 4 months pregnant, and I am worried sick that something happened to her baby.

She lowers her head in embarrassment and won't look me in the eyes. It takes a lot of coaxing, but she finally agrees to go with me upstairs to the bedroom. We sit down cross-legged on the floor as she sobs and pours her heart out to me.

With her broken English she chokes out, "Mrs. Peavy, I so ashamed." As Kalera calms down, she begins to tell me what happened. "Yesterday, I get home from work early. I open the door and one lady in bed with my husband Sai. Mrs. Peavy, I get crazy and start throwing things at them and screaming at her to get out of my house."

She continues to tell me, "Then Sai, he push me on the floor and start kicking and punching me. Mrs. Peavy, he punch my stomach." Now she puts her face in her hands and starts sobbing, "He punch my baby! My baby! Maybe something happen to my baby! And then he throw all my clothes and stuff out on the grass and set them on fire."

Kalera, our house girl

Hearing this, the blood is starting to rise to my face, and I am dumbfounded and angry. "Kalera, that's horrible. How dare he. It was his fault in the first place. And what about the baby? Doesn't he know that he could have killed the baby too?"

Her defensive response floors me. "Oh, no, Mrs. Peavy, it's my fault! It's all my fault. Not Sai's. I neva supposed to scream at him that way. I shame him in front of his lady friend."

110

"But Kalera, he was having sex with another woman. That's not ok!" I shouted, the blood continuing to rise to my face in anger.

"Mrs. Peavy, you don't understand. It's not his fault. Sai, he hasn't had sex for four months; see I can't have sex with him." She looks at me determinedly like this is an accepted fact.

"Kalera there is never any reason for someone to hurt you. And why can't you have sex with him?" I am trying to wrap my head around what she is saying. None of it makes any sense to me.

Kalera continues to cry softly. I could see this was eating her up inside. "If we have sex while baby in my tummy, the baby die. We women must turn our eye away and let our men do what they need to do because, well you know, they need it. You understand, right, Mrs. Peavy?" She looks at me with a face pleading for understanding.

I just stare at her in utter amazement. "What? Why can't you have sex with Sai? Who told you it would kill the baby? That's absolutely not true Kalera. Sex will not harm the baby at all. I've done it and all my friends do it. I promise it will not hurt the baby at all."

"Everyone knows that it will," she persisted. "The old women in the village, they always tell us that."

I spend another hour trying to convince her that her baby won't die if she has sex. But no matter what I say to convince her, she remains unwaveringly sure that the old women are right. And somehow at the end of our conversation, she still believes that she deserved the beating.

It is unfathomable to me that she can justify this beating. I haven't grown up in this culture where they are taught not to question what the elders in the village say. But Kalera has. And she has been taught not to question things for herself.

When we first got to Fiji, the missionaries told us that we should hire someone to help us with household duties and with the children. We quickly learned that most of the expat community did this because the menial tasks in a third world country were compounded and time consuming. They called these women that helped *house girls*, a term I had to learn to tolerate, as it sounded so demeaning. We ended up hiring and letting go a couple of women before we found Kalera.

Kalera lived a few miles down the road in a village where people still lived in huts made of grass or corrugated tin. We could hear their drum beats periodically throughout the day. Each beat had a different rhythm that signified specific events for the villagers throughout the day.

Kalera was in her early thirties, about the same age as I was at the time. She had grown up in a village near the interior of the island where life is still quite simple. Villages were usually built around a river because it provided drinking water, sanitation, and fishing for the people. Small individual huts made of thatched branches or corrugated tin were arranged around a large hut that would be used as the village meeting center.

The village was governed by a chief, called a Ratu. Every day, the Ratu and the men of the village sat together and decided which task each person would be appointed to do for the day. Some women would cook, others wash clothes, and others would take care of the children. For the most part, the men were sent out to gather food. Some hunted and some fished.

Fijians don't see individuality or the nuclear family as we see it in America. "It takes a village," is a mere saying here in the U.S., but is lived out perfectly in Fijian culture. I learned that their word for cousin was the same word used for brother or sister. The Fijian word for mother or father could be the same as for aunt or uncle.

Kalera explained it to me in her broken English. "Mrs. Peavy, we Fijians, we like big families. If you have many children, God bless you. Too sad if someone in your family can't have a baby. But no mind; a relative give them one of their babies. You Americans see family as Dad, Mum, and children. We see family as Uncle, Auntie, cousins, Boom Boom, Tutu (Grandma and Grandpa). If one of my babies die, my Auntie give me one of hers. We take care of each other."

A typical day in a village went like this. The drumbeat was the signal that directed their day. In the morning, the drums would call them to the central meeting place where they would talk about how they would divide up the daily chores. At the end of the day, the drumbeat would call them to come together for their last meal. Men first, women second, and children third. Afterwards, the women would clean up while the men and children played soccer, volleyball, or football out in the field. There was no such thing as a lonely villager. Everything was done together as one big family. I can't help but wonder if we Americans would be better off if we lived life the village way. I think our counseling centers would probably dry up.

The pastor of a large church in Suva explained it best. "I don't understand you Americans. Why do you need to be alone? You value such strange things like privacy and alone time. When I studied in America, I never even knew my neighbors. They would come home from work, drive in their driveway, and press their garage door open and then closed. I never even saw them. We didn't know each other. So, it puzzles me why you Americans say you're lonely and you pay to have friends. You buy gym memberships, join a country club, or go out to restaurants. Why don't you just stay outside and talk to your neighbors? You know, invite them into your homes, cook together, play ball outside with each other."

My responsibilities as a missionary were numerous. Our home was designated as the mission's house. We had various people stay with us for several months at a time the first year we were there. When a youth group would come on a short-term mission's trip, we were their connection to organize services and housing. If missionaries were passing through, our house was open for them to stay. I thoroughly enjoyed entertaining and getting to love on these visitors. Yet, sometimes I didn't feel I had enough time and energy to fulfill all my responsibilities to the best of my abilities. There was always so much going on. Add to that, we had two small children who were four and six years old.

Rusty and I taught classes at the Bible College. Our college was one of the three accredited Bible colleges in the South Pacific so islanders from all over the South Pacific attended our school.

Bible School Chapel Service

I taught whatever subject was needed at the time. Some of those classes I had never actually taken myself. A couple of times, I registered for the class and did online studies during the same calendar period I was teaching the class. Sometimes, I was just a lesson ahead of them, and hoped they wouldn't ask a question I couldn't answer. When it did happen, I'd just say, "Well, we'll get to that in a later lesson."

My American training had taught me that students learn best when they discover something for themselves. However, I quickly realized this wasn't a format that Fijians were comfortable with. Fijian schools are taught using the British system. The teacher teaches by rote and the students listen and regurgitate what they hear.

The first time I taught a course on Marriage and Family, I asked questions and waited...and waited...and waited. The students just weren't comfortable at all speaking out loud in class.

After many awkward quiet days in class, I thought, *There's got to be some way to get through to them. Think outside the box, Sherry, think.* And that's when an idea came to me. That night, Kalera and I baked a huge batch of chocolate chip cookies. The next day in class, I placed them on top of my desk, and told the students that whenever they answered a question, they could take a cookie. To my delight, from that day on, the class had many lively discussions.

During that course, we started discussing sexual relations within marriage. I decided to put a Pandora's Box in the library and told the students that they could anonymously write any questions they had and drop them in the box. As Rusty and I drove home after class a couple days later, I started unraveling the pieces of paper. To my surprise, there were a lot of questions. Some that pertained to highly sensitive sexual issues. At first, I thought this was going to turn into a disaster. How could we address these issues in a mixed group? We decided that Rusty would address the men, and I the women, in separate rooms. The discussions ended up gong really well and there was a lot of positive feedback afterwards.

Many other questions had to do with dating, even though this was a marriage and family class. We realized that this was an issue that was hushed and not talked about in Fiji. Romantic relationships were a new concept because of TV. Before this, it was cultural for the parents to pick their child's marriage partner. It was usually more of a monetary arrangement and had little to do with love.

Some of their questions about romantic relationships were:

"If I want to get to know a girl, how do I do it without everyone thinking I'm going to marry her?"

"If I like a boy, is it ok to kiss? How much touching can I do?"

"What if I like someone and my parents don't like him?"

"What if I like a girl, and then decide I don't like her later? Do I have to marry her?"

"Is it ok to be alone with each other?"

"Where can we be alone with each other?"

Rusty and I saw what an important, yet delicate subject this was and decided to address it. We began to do what we called, *Courting Seminars*. At these events, we talked about God's way of staying pure and getting to know someone of the opposite sex. I was somewhat

Me preaching in a Fijian church

apprehensive about what we would say. It felt as if we were sort of *writing the textbook* for Fijian Christian dating, and so much was at stake. I would like to think that we landed on a set of guidelines that was halfway between the old arranged marriages and the new American dating. For a while, we were asked to speak often on this topic. We put a lot of time and prayer into what we said, as we didn't want to offend their culture.

I realized early on that there was a preconceived idea that missionaries were somewhat next to God and were to be treated special. In Fiji, there is a pecking order, and it can be seen in the way people eat their meals. Most of the time, the men eat first, with the women serving and sometimes fanning them. I know that seems very male chauvinistic to us. But that is the way it still is in many parts of the world. When the men are finished eating, the women sit down and eat next, followed by the children who then get the leftovers.

Because I was both a missionary and a woman, meals were often a dilemma for me. Where should they seat me at these feasts? Even though I would always ask to be seated with the women, I would be politely guided to eat with the men. I didn't like that because for the most part I felt ignored. In the Fijian culture, a married man should not talk to or look at a married woman. Consequently, when I spoke, they would respond by looking at Rusty instead of me. It took a couple of years of my insistence, before the men felt comfortable seating me with the women.

On Sundays we spoke at various churches. Some of these were remote villages that could only be visited by canoe. When going to these villages, we would load the keyboard, sound system, and generator into a canoe and venture down the river. Some of these villages had never seen a white person before. The fact that the kids and I had white (blond) hair was a huge novelty.

Usually after the service, they prepared a feast

Canoeing to another island for Sunday service

for us. When I say feast, think of our large traditional Thanksgiving meal; more food than anyone could ever eat in one sitting. The meal usually consisted of a pig or cow that was smoked underground. This was quite a sacrifice, as villagers rarely ate meat because of the expense. One way to show that you enjoyed the meal, was to take seconds and thirds. The more you ate, the more they felt your gratitude.

I learned that being fat was a sign of beauty. It showed that your husband had enough wealth to take care of you. As such, I had to remind Kalera that whenever I gained a couple pounds, it was not okay for her to slap me on the butt and say, "Oh, Ms. Peavy you're getting so fat."

Rusty's grandpa visited Fiji for about a month each year. He absolutely loved preaching in the villages. As an old-time Pentecostal preacher, he would deliver fiery sermons, kicking his feet up in the air for effect. The Fijians loved that and they loved him. Fijian culture shows great respect to elderly people. Because Grandpa was in his mid-80's, they viewed him as next to God. The average life expectancy for a Fijian is somewhere in the mid-50's range. Grandpa was kind of an anomaly to them.

To show honor and respect, Fijian custom is that you speak softly and look down, never straight into the eyes of an elder. Well, Grandpa was pretty much deaf and going blind. So, when they would whisper to him, he would get annoyed, and would yell

"Huh?" More whispering. "Huh?" More of the quiet talking. "Huh? speak up, son, I can't hear ya." Then, when they would start talking louder, Grandpa would yell back, "Ok, ok. I heard ya the first time. You don't have to yell!" We thoroughly enjoyed these interactions.

To satisfy my social needs, I joined a women's group called The American Women's Club, comprised to expatriates (those who leave their home and live elsewhere, referred to world-wide as

expats). It was there that I formed some of my very closest friendships. We were each other's lifelines on everything from child rearing to celebrating American holidays. We also did our best to arrange American holiday

Our group of expat friends

events so that our kids wouldn't miss out on knowing their own culture. Not every holiday was included, but Christmas, Easter, 4th of July, Halloween, and Thanksgiving were among them.

Each Christmas, the whole town shut down for a month. Most everyone in Fiji would go back to their villages to be with their extended families. The seasons in Fiji are the exact opposite of the seasons in America. December is the hottest month of summer. While much of the world is singing *White Christmas* while shoveling snow, Fijians are singing *White Christmas* while on their white, sandy beaches.

Each Christmas we tried to do something special and unique to celebrate. One Christmas we took all the expat kids to an island by speedboat. My Dad, who was visiting for the holidays, dressed up like "Father Christmas," or as we call him, Santa Clause. Dad looked a lot like Colonel Sanders at the time, so he was a quite believable Santa Clause. He came by speedboat dressed in a full Santa suit shouting through a megaphone, "Ho Ho Ho! Merry

118

Christmas boys and girls!" As he sped by, he threw handfuls of candy to the kids on the shore.

He was a delightfully funny sight to see. The boat ride had sprayed him with water, and he was drenched from head to toe. The Santa suit hung wet and limp on this body. He came ashore and pulled the kids one by one onto his lap and asked them what they wanted for Christmas. When it

Dad, as Santa, with Melissa

came to Nathan's turn, he pulled my dad's beard down and loudly announced, "You're not Santa, you're my grandpa!" much to the kids' delight.

One Christmas we, along with several other expat families, stayed at a gorgeous resort for a few days. To try to create the Christmas spirit, we blacked out all our rooms' windows and turned the air conditioner on high until we convinced ourselves we were feeling somewhat frosty. On Christmas Eve, we decided it would be fun to go caroling down the hallways of our resort. Our missionary friend, Mark, had a guitar, so we all crammed into his *frosty* room and practiced as many Christmas songs as we knew; even adding some harmony parts.

One of our happy carolers was Terry, the regional director of Habitat for Humanity. He was close to seven feet tall and had been on a semi-pro basketball team in his younger years. Not only was he a giant in stature, but he also had a giant of a personality: gregarious and fun-loving. Terry had many talents; but singing wasn't one of them. However, this didn't seem to deter him from singing at the top of his lungs.

Christmas Eve came, and we all walked the resort halls singing joyous melodies of Christmas cheer. Some of the guests opened their doors to greet us, and some even joined us as we gleefully sang our songs down the hallways. The manager must have heard us singing and surprised us by asking if we would like to be the entertainment on stage that night at the dinner-house.

That night we stood proud and tall on stage singing our hearts out for the delighted hotel guests. Noone stood taller nor prouder than Terry. Towering over all of us in the back row, and beaming from ear to ear, he sang louder than all the rest of us combined. He told us later that he had always dreamed of singing in front of a crowd of people. That was one of the precious things about Fiji, we were all big fish in a small pond.

Another Christmas, we invited a large group of friends to join us for a Christmas talent show that we called *Carols by Candlelight*. This was an event that Rusty and I had led at every church we had been a part of. We would darken the sanctuary, and light candles from every possible place. The sanctuary would glow as participants sang, played an instrument, put on a skit, or expressed any other talent they possessed. Between acts, I played the piano, and those that gathered sang Christmas carols. The night concluded with everyone sharing the cookies they had brought to share.

We decided this would be a fun festivity to host in Fiji as well. Everyone came bundled up in their sweaters and scarves. The air conditioner was set on high and pumping out the coldest air possible. The sweet aromas of cookies and other baked goods wafted in the air. One by one, each family shared their talents for the group. The children taking instrument lessons blessed us with their beautiful, and not so beautiful, selections. One year, the crowd favorite was the Hillbilly rendition of *Jingle Bells*, sung by the Wakefield family from Georgia. With their blackened-out teeth, overalls, and straw hats they sang their selection complete with their perfect crooner-drawl. Mark, the dad, strummed along with his stand-up base.

For our 4th of July celebrations, we ordered hot dogs from America, and had a family park day, consisting of baseball, hot dogs, patriotic songs, and fireworks display to top it off. It's funny how nostalgic and patriotic we become when we're far from home. I probably felt more patriotic while in Fiji than at any other time in my life.

Halloween turned out to be a hoot. We brought candy to our neighbors and tried to explain to them that kids in crazy costumes would be knocking at their door in the evening to receive candy handouts. Although most of them thought this was quite strange, they complied with our request and the kids had a lot of fun. I think these holidays were almost more special to us because we were away from our culture and extended families. It brought a sense of the familiar to our lives overseas, where everything around us was so different.

I joined a ladies' group that consisted mostly of Aussies (Australians) and Kiwis (New Zealanders). I can't remember any other Americans while there; I soon found out why. Their home cultures made these gatherings uncomfortable for Americans. Down under, they have a saying called *Toppin' off the poppy*. The premise is that all the poppy flowers need to be the same height. If one is taller, it should be chopped down. If one is shorter, it should be elevated. In other words, if one woman is perceived better in anyway, richer, or more beautiful, the others will look down on her because that is unacceptable. And the opposite is true as well. If a woman is a plain Jane, poor, or in any way less than the rest of the ladies, she will be elevated and lifted.

I had no idea that this was a *thing* in their countries. Coming from America where people take great strides to be better, it seemed very odd to me. It's interesting how each one of us is affected greatly by the subliminal beliefs of the culture where we are raised.

Two ladies in the group befriended me. Linda, from England, and Tess, from New Zealand. We were all crazy enough to laugh at our cultural differences. They told me that because I wore makeup and had big blond hair, the women looked at me as trying to be better than them. Remember, all the poppies must be the same, so they set about to bring me down. You better believe that after that, I would attend their functions in the frumpiest thing I could wear and a bare face. I never could quite pat the hair down though.

A few of us Christian ladies from these groups began a weekly Bible Study. We saw God do some amazing miracles. Several gave their hearts to Christ and still others grew to accept the differences in our denominations. It is still interesting to think of how close our relationships grew during that time. We were all so very different, and if we had met in our own cultures, would probably not even be friends. However, because we were living abroad and away from our comfort zones, the similarities we shared were greater than our differences. We grew to love each other very much. Most of those ladies live in different parts of the world today, but we stay in touch and get together when we can.

One of things that brought me real joy was helping get the Missionette program grounded in Fiji. This program is a Christian girls' club very similar to the Girl Scouts. It has been around since the 1960's when I was a part of the program. Girls come together

Missionette Board

each week wearing their uniforms. They work together to earn badges and awards by studying the Bible and learning practical skills. At the end of the 4–year program, a girl is grounded in the Word of God and given a solid foundation to live a well-rounded life physically, mentally, and spiritually.

As the program in Fiji grew, we formed a board of ladies to facilitate and maintain it. At that time, the Missionettes in America were just switching to newer uniforms and manuals. We wrote home and asked if they would like to donate their outdated supplies to the Fijian girls. They agreed and this ended up being a huge blessing for the girls in Fiji. They were delighted to have these new-to-them treats. It was a joy to watch them march proudly into a Missionette rally wearing their uniforms with the badges they had earned pinned to their vests.

Secure at Last

Chapter 14
992—1997

Scary Times

I am having this burst of memories as I'm currently in a village teaching women at a three-day conference. My mind is vibrant with the image I had three years ago back in the States. And now as I live it in real life experience, my heart is filled with amazement and joy.

The women come hungry and look at me expecting God to speak through me. *Oh God, let every word I say be straight from Your Holy Spirit. Fill these women's hearts with Your truth and presence. Let me be invisible so that You may be seen!* My heart prays fervently for these beautiful women.

I came back to Suva from this mountain top experience, energized in Spirit but sick in body. There had been a virus circulating in the village and apparently it got me too. I lay in bed the first few days expecting to get better and back to my normal life soon.

However, when the sickness didn't go away within the normal 4-6 days, I began to wonder if it had gone into an infection. After some tests, the doctor concluded that I didn't have a bacterial infection so there was nothing they could do to help. I chalked it up to being over-tired from a hectic schedule. It was Christmas break, and I figured if I took the holiday break and rested, my body would be back to normal when school started again.

However, the symptoms continued to drag on for weeks and then even into months. I was achy from head to toe and extremely exhausted. My brain felt cloudy, I had a sore throat, swollen glands, and a mild fever. I lay in bed literally unable to do anything, wondering why I wasn't getting better, and begging God to heal me so I could get up and do more work for Him. I remember bargaining with Him, challenging Him, shouting at Him, with nothing but a blank ceiling staring back at me. No response and no healing. Nothing! I was frustrated, confused, and depressed. What good was I doing lying there incapacitated when there was so much good to be done if I was well?

I had some things to learn during that time. To begin with: God isn't as concerned about *what I do* as much as *who I am*. My entire life, I had thought that pleasing God was *doing* something for Him. Sure, I knew it was because of His grace that He forgave my sins and made me His child. But once I was a Christian, wasn't *doing* good things for God the most important thing I could do on earth? I tended to equate how much I was doing for Him with how much He was pleased with me.

Because our culture, including church culture, usually has focused its teachings more on how to *do* and not as much on how to *be*, we tend to fill our God-hungry, empty spaces with activities. It's so much easier to bring snacks for Sunday School than to spend time on our knees in the prayer room. We can become so busy with church life that there's no time for God. Doing *God's work* can bring about so much satisfaction and recognition that we begin to exalt the work more than God Himself.

God wants us to first find fulfillment in a rich inner life relationship with Him. Then out of that, to let our service for Him flow. The service is about our relationship with God, and not about our need to be needed. He wants our satisfaction to come not from a job well done, but from being a child of God that is well-loved.

During this abrupt halt in my activities, I seriously questioned what good I was to God. Since He had forgiven me, I felt like the dutiful older brother in the Prodigal Son story. I was going about my Father's business. Surely that was better than being incapacitated and accomplishing nothing, right?

But through these months on my back, I began to realize that *being* God's much-loved child was more important to God. I still felt broken, but somehow hopeful. It seemed as if God were wringing all that self-sufficiency out of me and asking that I just find my joy and worth in being His child. Walking or lying down, doing or being. He was all about molding my character; not so concerned with what I could do for Him.

He also led me to study the scripture that says, *the good that God has for you to do, do it.* I'd always been the kind of person that thought if there was an opportunity to do something good, I should do it. Statistics show that 20% of people do 80% of the work in church. I was in that 20%.

God was trying to say to me that there is good for everyone to do. When I do somebody else's good, I rob them from being needed and blessed. And I also burn myself and my body out and end up being no good to anyone. We get overwhelmed when we try to do everyone's good. God has given each of us our own good things to do. Let's not try doing *all* the good—just our own good.

After three months of being sick in bed, we decided we needed to seek medical help elsewhere. If the doctors in Fiji couldn't diagnose my situation, I would have to return to the States. Our leaders authorized me to fly to Stanford Hospital in California, where they put me through a battery of tests. They found an unusually high amount of T cells in my body, and after more testing, diagnosed me with *Chronic Fatigue Syndrome*, an auto immune suppressed disease. I know there seems to be a lot of people out there who have been wrongly diagnosed with these kinds of diseases. It seems that when doctors can't find anything else to pin a patient's symptoms on, they put it in this category.

However, I could have been the pinup poster child for CFS. Every symptom and the way I came down with it was spot on. The doctor started me on an antidepressant called Sinequan. He told me I would need to alter my lifestyle for quite a while to get better. It ended up being a full year before I was able to return to normal life.

I wish I could say that I was healed of it. But sadly, I still have that disease today. Most of the time it's in remission, but when I overdo it or am stressed and exhausted, my body lets me know. It's like a barometer ticking inside that won't allow me to fake my way through exhaustion anymore. This disease keeps me from pushing my body over its limits. The epicenter of the pain starts in the right side of my chest. When I feel that, I know I must stop, cancel everything, and rest. I guess for too many years, I ran on fumes and kept running and running like a mouse on a wheel. Now I see myself more as a cautious cat that knows my boundaries and must stick to them.

Although I lived with CFS all through our remaining years in Fiji, God did perform some other amazing miracles for our family. Melissa came down with a scary disease. One day, she came inside from playing and complained that her neck hurt. She was crying and said that she had a bad headache. She then proceeded to curl up in a little ball on the floor while her temperature rose to an alarming 105 degrees. When a rash broke out all over her body, we quickly realized something was very wrong and rushed her to the doctor.

Secure at Last

Melissa was diagnosed with Hemorrhagic Dengue Fever; a form of malaria spread through mosquitos. This type of Dengue is very dangerous, and often kills young children and elderly people. The doctor explained, "The scary part of this particular strain of the disease is that if she bumps into something, she could bleed internally and die. Normally the symptoms last for six months. Another side effect we see often is that the patient can go blind."

Although I seem to handle other stresses alright, when it comes to something traumatic happening to one of my children, I completely freak out. When the doctor explained that Melissa could die or go blind, I ended up passing out flat on the floor! When we got home, I immediately contacted our prayer chain in the U.S. and asked for urgent prayer. That was a hard night, releasing my precious girl into God's hands.

The scariest part of agreeing to work overseas for me had always been the fear of something happening to one of our children. God heard the prayers of His saints all over the country as well as this freaked out mama. The next day, to our surprise and relief, she began rallying around and eating. Three days later, Melissa was free of symptoms and back in school. Absolutely a miracle with no explanation but God! There are no words to describe our relief and thankfulness for God's supernatural intervention for her.

Another scary time was when our son Nathan had an accident with a wheelbarrow. I was working from home when I heard blood curdling screams coming from down the street. I ran outside and saw the neighbor kids running towards the house carrying Nathan in their arms. "Oh my gosh, you guys, what happened?" I screamed.

Nathan's leg was bleeding profusely and there was a huge, jagged gash all around his knee. I could see layers of shredded flesh. It seemed that his leg was barely dangling from the bone. Everyone seemed to be talking at once. "We were playing with the wheelbarrow. Probesh was inside it and Nathan was pushing him really fast down the street. I think he couldn't stop, because he ran into the curb going really fast. The wheelbarrow just stopped, and

Nathan's leg ran into that jagged part. He's going to be alright right, Mrs. Peavy?"

My heart leaped with the horrid thought that he might lose his leg. Nathan was screaming repeatedly, "Mom, am I going to die? Am I going to die?" I think I was just as freaked out and scared as he was, but I tried to act strong for his sake. After wrapping his leg very tightly in gauze, I called all our private doctors. Nobody was answering. It suddenly dawned on me that it was Fiji Day, a national public holiday. The only place to find help was at the hospital, which the Fijians morbidly called the *Vale Ne Mate*, translated *The House of Death*. Let's just say nobody wants to go there.

With no other choice, we quickly drove him to the hospital and checked in. A large woman took him into a room with me right on her trail; she had to forcefully push me out of the room. I don't know what she did in there, but there was a lot of screaming coming from the room, and my mama-heart felt every bit of the pain I heard Nathan going through. It felt like hours when she finally came out of the room and told us that she had put in over 100 stitches – a layer on the inside and on the outside.

For the next three months, Nathan's leg had infection after infection that just wouldn't heal. My poor little buddy. Ultimately, a specialist opened the wound back up to drain out the infection. He decided it was best to leave it open for optimal healing. Because of this, to this day, Nathan has a gnarly jagged scar that goes almost all the way around his kneecap. On quite a few occasions, he's been known to tell a little different version of how he got the scar. His version? A shark attack.

Chapter 15
1997

Crossroads

"Wow! We've been all over the world and I've never seen anything like this," I exclaimed to Rusty as the taxi drove us through the streets of Manila, Philippines. "There are cars everywhere. I mean look at this lane. There are two cars in it. Look over there.

Normal traffic in Manilla

Cars are even on the sidewalk. People walking in the middle of the cars. And look at all these rickshaws winding around the traffic. How are these people not getting killed?"

Our car slows as we near the mission house. "Whew, we made it!" Rusty exclaims as we open the door and get out of the car. Immediately, we are completely overwhelmed by the thick grey cloud of exhaust that fills the air. My chest constricts and tightens as I try to take a breath.

"So glad Cina told us to bring masks. Who knew it was this bad?" I say as we quickly maneuver the straps around our ears.

A few days later, I'm sitting in a restaurant waiting for my childhood friend Cina to join me. In my mind I recount all the activities of the last few days. *We've been accepted as the new Pastors of the English-speaking International Church here in Manila; we got the kids enrolled in the International Mission's School, we found a house and even hired a house girl. The doors seem to be wide open to us moving here!*

My thoughts are interrupted as my friend Cina comes bustling through the door. "Hey sweetie!" we both say at the same time and laugh. It's been years, and I'm thrilled to see my old familiar friend. She had been my babysitter when I was in elementary school. Over the years we had developed a friendship since she was just a few years older than I. Cina and her husband Tye had been missionaries in the Philippines for years.

I motion for her to sit beside me and begin to eagerly fill her in on our plans to move to Manila. Like excited school children, we catch each other up on our lives as we eat our sandwiches and salads. At one point she asks me if I'm ok to eat salad from a street vendor and I assure her that my stomach is like steel. "Are you kidding? I'm the only one in my family who hasn't been affected by giardia," a water bacterium.

"Oh good" she replies. "Some people get really sick when they eat from vendors on the street. Hey, do you want me to take you on a tour of the city? Did you know we have the biggest mall in the world here? It's called the Mile Long Mall."

"Are you kidding?" I exclaim. "That's my kind of shopping. Let's do it!"

Somewhere in the middle of the seemingly endless rows of stores, my stomach starts speaking to me with grumbling and gurgling sounds. Realizing that the bathroom is quite a long way away, I tell Cina that I will be right back and sprint my way through hallways.

Finally arriving at the destination, a maid starts to tell me that the bathroom is closed. "Right!" I say as I whiz by her and slam the door of the stall. Have you ever heard of Montezuma's Revenge? Let's put it this way; I made it just in time.

Hours later, with fever, chills, and many more trips to the commode, I am lying on the mission's bed sweating profusely. *Shoot, I have the stomach flu!* I sadly muse. *I hope this doesn't last long. We've got to get on a plane and get back to the kids in a couple days.*

My fever keeps climbing quickly and for the next three days, I am one with the toilet and shower. It is some of the worst pain I've ever experienced – seriously up there with childbirth. On the third day I begin bleeding from every orifice of my body, and my fever is so high that my body begins to go into shock. I don't know this at the time, but my body is bleeding internally.

"Jesus, Jesus, Jesus" is all I can whisper as I shake violently on the bed. The sheets are completely soaked, and my body convulses so strong that Rusty has gone to the floor to sleep. At one point in the night, I find my conscious self going up towards the ceiling. I look down at my body as a casual observer. It's so very strange, but I am not surprised or fearful. In fact, I am devoid of any feeling about my body. It's lying limply on the bed. I can see Rusty asleep on the floor.

The next thing that happens is surreal. Individual beams of light start going down and hitting my lifeless body. I notice that each beam has a word inside it. The word-beams are flowing in rapid succession into my body and as they do, I start to see that they are forming entire verses of scriptures that I memorized as a child. As

133

these word-beams enter my lifeless body, it's as if they are feeding it something that brings it back to life again. I return to my body, only to have it happen again and again. This happens several times throughout the night.

Somewhat surprised to still be alive the next morning, I try to relay to Rusty and the mission's staff what happened. Immediately they contact a doctor who comes to the house that morning. He gives me medication and does multiple tests confirming that I have E Coli. Apparently, it was from the lettuce on the salad I had eaten with my friend. I start the antibiotic treatment and within 24 hours I am feeling so much better. Sadly, we have to postpone our return for a few days until I am able to regain enough strength to fly back to Fiji. I miss my kids so much!

When we finally got back to Fiji, we started questioning the wisdom of moving to Manila. That had been a very serious battle for my life. I did what I always do when I have a hard decision to make; I sat down and wrote a list of pros and cons. Considering the possibility that this was Satan trying to keep us from going to the Philippines, my instinct was to fight back and go.

Before making that final decision, we decided to write to ten couples we trusted and ask them for their wisdom in the matter. To our amazement, all ten wrote back and counseled us not to go. The gist of what they said was: *We encourage you strongly not to go! Sherry's system can't take the pollutants in Manila, and you'll end up burying her there.*

Wow! That was not what we expected to hear, and it stopped us in our tracks.

We called the Manila church leaders and told them that we had changed our minds about coming. Now we were scratching our heads about where our next steps should take us. We voiced this to our leaders back in the U.S. This prompted a call inviting us to take a new position in Southern California overseeing the denomination's ethnic churches there. This seemed to be tailor-made for Rusty, as he loved third world cultures. We accepted the invitation, and soon we were winding up our ministry in Fiji, packing, saying our goodbyes, and heading back to America.

Once we arrived in California, we found a house to rent not far from Rusty's family, got the kids enrolled in school, and Rusty started his new job. It was obvious we couldn't survive on the monthly support we had been getting in Fiji, so I started looking for teaching positions. I ended up teaching music at two schools as well as doing private piano lessons at home.

For the first time, Nathan and Melissa were attending a public school; Nathan in seventh grade and Melissa in sixth. Both were academically in way over their heads for a while. Fijian private school was run like a tight ship, using the British method of teaching. The students behaved or else they got smacked on the head or flicked on the ear. Orange County public school was like going to a party where everyone dressed in the latest surf brands. How *cool* you were considered was based on how defiant you could be to the teacher.

The transition from the town life of Fiji to the bustling cities of Southern California was like moving to a different planet. This was evidenced when one of the churches blessed each of our kids with gift certificates to Toys R Us. The kids had so much fun looking in the store. They started shopping on one side and worked their way around to the other side, amazed at all the options. However, when they finally got to the checkout aisle, their carts were still empty. They were simply too overwhelmed to make a choice. We left without buying a single thing. Of course, this never happened again. They quickly adjusted to their new Southern California lifestyle.

For various reasons during this time, Rusty and I had a bit of a role reversal. He had returned to America with some health issues. Because of this, I began making many of the household decisions, which I discovered was an enjoyable change for me. We stayed in Southern California for two years and loved being so close to Rusty's wonderful family. However, we found ourselves easily falling into the hustle bustle lifestyle, and in time we were overwhelmed with busyness like everyone around us. Realizing that this was a much faster lifestyle than we wanted for our family, we began to look for ministry opportunities in the slower paced Northern California region.

Back home to the USA

The job that was best suited for Rusty ended up being the very same position he was serving in but based in Northern California instead. The headquarters were based in Sacramento. This was a great choice for the family as it was back in our old stomping grounds near many of our old friends and some of my family.

The move to Northern California felt like a move home, so it was an easy and comfortable transition. We bought a house, enrolled the kids in a large Christian School, and started our new life. With Rusty's last position, we had traveled and held services in various churches on the weekends. Consequently, the kids hadn't had a home church for a long time. We decided it would be good for them to get involved in a church of their own, so the kids and I began attending the church that sponsored their school.

We needed some extra financial help, so I asked the kids' school if I could start a piano program there. Kids would come out of class for a half hour piano lesson each week. The school agreed, and this program turned out to be beneficial to everyone involved. The parents didn't have to transport their kids back and forth to lessons, and I kicked back a portion of what I earned to the school music program. As an extra bonus, some of the students ended up playing for the Jr. and Sr. high school chapel band. I joined the church band and started playing the piano for the services on Sundays as well. This was the first time I had ever played along with a live orchestra, and I thoroughly enjoyed it.

However, one Sunday morning, I had quite a comical experience at the piano. If you know music, you'll get a kick out of this. There were about 2,000 people in the congregation. I was playing the grand piano on the left side of the platform with the live orchestra playing on the right side. During the offering, the choir was singing a beautiful song with quite a few key changes that built in intensity. One of them happened to be right after a page turn.

When I tried to flip the page, the whole book went flying off the piano stand and onto the floor. Of course, this wasn't my first rodeo. Usually, I would just wing it and continue playing by ear. But I wasn't sure of the next key or even of how the song sounded, so there was absolutely no way to fake it. I had no other choice than to simply stop playing. The choir and the orchestra completely lost their notes and froze while the choir director looked at me like a deer in the headlights. Mortified, I fumbled down on the floor trying to retrieve the book. We did finally get back on track, but those few seconds seemed like an eternity.

The next few years of teaching and playing piano at this mega church were busy and fulfilling. However, there was also a storm brewing beneath my marriage. You see, I had major unresolved issues that I had stuffed down for many years. I had only revealed them to a select few. To everyone else, our marriage was exemplar on the surface.

I must reveal here that this next paragraph is probably the hardest I've had to write. Because of the sensitive nature of this subject, I'm not going to give many details. As in all marriages, there are struggles and many have difficulties. However, my way of dealing with them was to cover them up. I chose not to address them. Instead, I closed my heart to protect it. I can't say how that was possible. But I managed to smile on the outside and pretend that everything was fine. I practiced the art of *covering up,* a skill I totally hated, but felt was necessary for emotional safety and survival.

I remember many years prior during our honeymoon and ministry trip to Europe, the evangelist's wife traveling with us had given me a small lecture about this very thing. She had seen my swollen red eyes that night and had noticed that I wasn't participating in singing during the worship time that Rusty was leading. She pulled me aside and asked if he and I had been in a quarrel. I sullenly admitted that we had. She looked at me straight in the eyes and said, "Sherry, the people coming to these meetings expect us to be strong and able to bear their burdens. You just need to buck up, put your feelings aside, and be a good actress until you get home."

"I will never do that," I told her emphatically. "That is just being a hypocrite and living a lie."

However here I was many years later and an expert at it. I kept all those hurtful feelings bottled up inside and became a dutiful puppet, saying and doing the things that looked proper as a minister's wife. Once in a great while, those feelings would surface and when they did, I would explode like a pent-up volcano. Afterwards I would feel horrible and ask for forgiveness in order to go on living *my righteous life.*

I remember a night when some longtime friends who knew me well took me aside and asked if I was ok. They said that I appeared to be a shell of the person I had been, and they were concerned that I had lost myself. I just smiled and said what I had been saying for years, "I'm fine, really, I am. I've just had to adapt to ministry, but we're doing great. Thanks for your concern."

Now here I was, facing the reality that I *had* lost myself. I really *was* a shell of a person. My usual zest and enthusiasm for life had faded. I had grown good at shielding my heart and hiding my real feelings. I had lived an emotionally even-keeled life when it came to my marriage; figuring that if I didn't feel, there would be no pain and I'd be fine. I wasn't fine. We sought counseling and I desperately hoped things would change. But as I began to see the truth about our lives, the more I knew something had to change or I would lose myself completely.

I didn't believe then that divorce was an option, and still don't advocate it. I had meant my marriage vows. I thought of myself as a woman with high character. I believed strongly in the power of

God to heal broken lives and to heal marriages. Let me say here, that I strongly hate divorce and understand why God does as well. It is hard on everyone involved, and marriage should be pursued at all costs. Both individuals must be willing to put in hard work every day for healing to occur.

I learned something imperative about relationships through this marital struggle. Bottling up feelings and living a lie will emotionally kill you. Even though I felt that those who looked up to us as role models would be disillusioned, I was wrong to live a life of pretense.

If this is you, I beg you, please do not do what I did! If your relationship is not built on truth, it will decay and eventually crumble. There is a healthy way to express anger and frustration, hurt and disappointment. There are many good books for those of us with the tendency to bottle up our feelings. We can learn how to express our feelings and encourage healthy conversations that lead to discussions instead of explosions.

We all have faults and weaknesses. If we can be honest about them, we can work towards healing and growth. Without honesty, we are stuck and cannot grow. Along with honesty, we need to be willing to change, listen, and grow. It takes courage to admit we are wrong. And courage to forgive. I've been told that two forgivers make a great marriage. I have found this to be so true!

It was a difficult situation to navigate through, and many, many tears were shed. Splitting apart an 18-year marriage with children is extremely difficult and brings many challenges, especially when you are in the church spotlight. We gave Nathan and Melissa the choice of where they wanted to live.

Nathan chose to stay in the house with Rusty, and Melissa chose to move with me into a woman's house where I rented two rooms. The woman we rented from lived in the house as well. It turned out that she was a Christian marriage therapist. She recommended many books for me to read and as it turned out, I received many free and spontaneous counseling sessions right there in her kitchen.

These were hard years of change and growth. I used this time to work on me and my issues. We usually want to blame the other person for a divorce. But when it all boils down to it, it takes two. We can't change the other person, but we can put in the work to change ourselves and become the best possible version of who we are. I read everything I could get my hands on that dealt with my issues. I also continued going to a therapist who gave me great insight into myself and the necessary steps to take for healing and growth.

Having been married for almost 20 years, I felt a little awkward suddenly becoming a single person. It was like a three-legged dog having to adjust to a missing leg. *Divorcee*, such an ugly word; a word I had not planned for myself. What was the older single woman's place and role supposed to look like? As I watched other single men and women, I began to understand how lonely life's road can be for them.

Those singles who were around my age (40ish) seemed to suffer to some degree with emotional damage, baggage, and or strange idiosyncrasies. I could sense the brokenness and sometimes even strange behavior in a lot of my new, single friends. For many, their worlds had come crashing down. My own life was a paradox of grief and uncertainty as well as a newfound freedom to be myself all mixed together.

I was still working at the school and playing piano at the church. It seemed Melissa and I were at the campus more than we were home. I even kept a rollup mat in my classroom closet so that I could take naps when needed. Between Melissa's school and afterschool sports programs, and my teaching and piano playing schedule, we were there every day and many nights. The church had become our home away from home. It felt comfortable there. That is, until the divorce.

When the news spread about the marital split, some people began treating me differently. At first, I thought maybe it was just in my head. In time it became apparent that there were quite a few people that were extremely judgmental about our divorce. Some that I had regularly chatted with while walking the hallways of our church, began to turn their faces away when I walked by.

I already felt enough disgrace and failure of my own, this just amplified it. I began walking with my head down, trying not to make eye contact with anyone to escape the judging eyes and murmuring lips. I heard from well-meaning friends some of the things being said about me, and it hurt to my core. Early on, I had decided not to disclose any of our struggles as it would do more harm than good. I paid a price for remaining silent, but still feel it was the right thing to do.

It's strange, when someone in the church falls, it tends to make some feel somewhat better about themselves. *Well, we may not have the perfect marriage, but at least we're not divorced.* Chewing on other people's failures can give us a sense of pride. *At least we're not as bad off as they are.* So, we pull ourselves away out of our sense of indignity. We become so focused on their extensive list of shortcomings, that we can't see God's mercy and love that should be poured out to them.

This is so sad. It is exactly the opposite of what a suffering Christian needs in their time of pain. The wounded person desperately needs others to see their bleeding heart, to have others come alongside their wounded soul, and to find God's outpouring love. The one place where God's people should embrace the broken hearted is the church. It's as though a soldier has been wounded in battle, but instead of coming alongside and offering help and healing, many times more arrows are thrown, and even greater damage is done. In their insecurity and harshness, some church members kick those who are already down, wounded and broken.

I don't want to give the impression that everything in my life during that period was horrible. There were also new friendships forged and others strengthened. Melissa's friends and their moms became priceless to us. We hosted frequent pool parties and sleepovers. We remain close to many of these now grownup girls and their mamas to this day. I am so thankful for each one of them.

Through the years, Rusty and I have remained in contact. We are truly friends. He often joins us for holidays and extended family gatherings.

Chapter 16
'2003

Melissa's Fight for Health

Sitting in the bleachers at the 2003 Regional Cheerleading Competition, I, along with the other girls' moms, am nervously awaiting our team's name to be called.

Finally, the loudspeaker booms, "And next up, we have the Capital Christian School Junior Varsity squad. CCS boasts a three-year championship in their division. Let's give it up for CCS!"

We moms stand up and scream without abandon for our girls' entrance! Here they come, each with hair coifed into a perfect ponytail under their big blue ribbon. "CCS, CCS, CCS, Whooooo

143

go girls!" we scream in unison feeling every nerve-racking jitter they must be feeling.

The arena quiets and we sit down, hearts pounding with nervous excitement for them. We know they have all the tricks to wow the judges, but can they pull it off?

Melissa's cheerleading squad

The music starts, and the girls move in perfect unison as they have been doing in the proceeding hours of countless practices. My heart is swelling with pride as I nervously pick at my nails. Of course, my eyes are locked in on my girl Melissa. *We're halfway there, girls. You got this!* I think as the seconds feel like minutes.

All of a sudden, my heart skips a beat. *What's that? Is that vomit? Oh my gosh, my girl is projectile vomiting!* My eyes are glued to her like a Mama Bear. I watch in pain as she never stops or misses a beat of the routine. Somehow, she and the girls continue to finish flawlessly even while she continues to vomit.

The routine finishes and the girls run to exit the outside door. My Mama heart is beating wildly as I run behind them to find my daughter. As I come outside to the courtyard, I see all of the girls except for Melissa.

I find her in a dark corner. She's in a heap on the floor crying. I fall on the ground beside her, take her into my arms, and let her weep. "It's ok sweetheart, it's ok." I gently stroke her hair as she continues to weep.

"I ruined everything, Mom. I let everybody down. It's all my fault!" All I can do is hold her and tell her it will all be ok.

"Babe, you did your best! I am so proud of you. And look how you never even skipped a beat. You just kept going. You did a fabulous job!"

Amazingly, their squad still won first place! We spent the next day playing at Disneyland, and it seemed like everything was back to normal. We drove back home the following day to start the school and work week. In my thinking, what happened to Melissa was just a moot point that was unfortunate, but no big deal. However, on Friday morning I got a call from Melissa's cell phone. She was crying and terribly upset. She mumbled through her tears, "Mom you have to come get me right now. I'm in the bathroom at school. The squad is doing the same Disneyland routine for pep rally, and I just can't go out there." I tried to talk her out of her fear, but no amount of talking eased her anxiety. She wasn't going to do it.

When I brought her home, she was incredibly anxious and withdrawn. For the next few days, Melissa didn't want me out of her sight. She followed me everywhere and even wanted to sleep with me at night. I wanted so badly to take away her pain and anxiety, but nothing I said or did seemed to help. Slowly she improved and was able to go back to school, although every once in a while, she would have another panic attack.

One Wednesday night Melissa came home from youth group an emotional mess. Their youth leader had suddenly died that morning in a diving accident. Apparently, he had taken some kids with him to swim in a lake. Tragically, while diving he hit his head on a rock and was instantly killed. Melissa was devastated. That night while I was sleeping, she came into my room sobbing and said that there was a voice in her head telling her to take the knives in the kitchen and kill herself. She genuinely believed that if she were alone, the voice would prevail and make her do the unthinkable.

She slept with me that night, and in the morning was still seized with panic and fear that the voice in her head would prevail. The morning turned into evening and into days, and then weeks. She couldn't be alone. My sweet daughter went to work with me, slept in my room, and was terribly afraid to be around people, the total opposite of her normal personality. The voice telling her to kill herself would not go away.

We dealt with it spiritually, thinking it was the enemy tormenting her. We talked, prayed, and sought counseling, but nothing seemed to give her relief. Trying rational thinking and mind over matter were not taking any of the thoughts away. It's horrible when you can't help your child's suffering and don't have any idea where to turn to find answers.

We finally went to a psychiatrist to seek medical intervention. She prescribed an antidepressant and sent us to a psychologist who diagnosed Melissa with OCD, Obsessive Compulsive Disorder, and panic attacks. We were given a workbook to help us work through the issues. It listed many helpful steps on what to do when she felt a panic attack coming on. One of the steps was to breathe slowly in through her nose and out through her mouth. Another step suggested engaging in strenuous physical exercise to use up some of the nervous energy. It also taught a new way to talk to herself. Besides using these techniques, we tried a few antidepressants until we found one that worked wonders for her. She began to sleep better; the voice in her head finally faded and eventually stopped completely. The panic attacks subsided.

Today, Melissa continues taking medication for anxiety. She has quit taking them three different times because of pregnancy. However, after the babies were born, the anxiety seemed to return.

Fighting anxiety together

She has resolved that taking the medication greatly helps her keep the anxiety under control and to live a healthy life. This is not a sign of weakness but an understanding that medication fills a gap where something is missing in the brain. Much like a physical sickness, like insulin does for diabetics. It is a mental ailment where the brain has a medical need.

I too, have taken an antidepressant for 25 years that keeps the Auto Immune Disease, Chronic Fatigue Syndrome, under control. I want to suggest that it is wise to seek out medical help when nothing else works. With our increasingly stressful world, more and more people suffer from depression and anxiety. It is nothing to be ashamed of. If this is you, please reach out and get help. Melissa would tell you herself that it has helped give her a healthy balanced life. She lives life fully, managing her successful influencer business, three active little ones, and sustaining a healthy marriage and social life.

I asked Melissa if she wanted to add to this story from her perspective, and she eagerly approved of it as written. Her desire has always been to be honest and transparent about her life if it helps other people with similar challenges. I believe much of Melissa's blogging success stems from how honest and real she is about her life. (Ellabrooksblog)

Ella Marie, Jude, Brooklyn,
Melissa, and Travis Cole

Secure at Last

Chapter 17
2007—2013

Love and Betrayal

Oh, my goodness! Where is the darn restaurant? I've been up and down this street three times and it's not here! If meeting a strange man wasn't already nerve racking enough, I realize that I am already ten minutes late.

There it is! Finally, I see it. The restaurant sign is tucked under the branches of an overhanging tree. Feeling relieved, I find a place to park, and start walking down the sidewalk. As the front door of the restaurant comes into view, I notice a tall, dark, and handsome man leaning up against the front of the building. *Oh wow, I hope he's my date!* My heart skips a beat or two.

Secure at Last

Our eyes meet as I reach the restaurant. He smiles and cocks his head sideways. "Hi, are you Sherry?" he asks with a boyish grin. "Yes, that's me. And you must be Kevin?" I quickly answer matching his smile.

He opens the door for me as we walk inside. Sitting down at a table, I notice how broad his shoulders are and how adorable his dimples are when he smiles, which is often. His demeanor is soft but rugged at the same time. I realize that I am going to enjoy myself very much this evening.

We quickly engage in conversation starting with the broad stories of who we are and where we come from; and then move into more depth and meaningful details of our lives. The conversation is easy, and we laugh quite often. The fondue is an amazing array of meats and vegetables with varying dipping sauces exploding with flavor. The wine he pairs with the food blends well. I am enjoying myself immensely. Kevin hushes his voice and begins to soberly tell me something that he thinks I should know.

"Sherry, I don't know how you feel about this. I would love to continue to get to know you further. But first I need to share something with you that could be a deal breaker."

I blink back a couple of times. "Ok, what's that?" I eagerly lean forward trying to anticipate what he will say.

"Well, I have a disease that will continue to be with me all of my life. It's cancer." I swallow hard as he continues to talk. "I was diagnosed with it a few years ago and went through some chemo down in Texas for about 4 months. Lost my hair and was pretty sick for a while. But the good news is that I can live a rather normal life with ongoing radiation treatments."

"Wow that's really good news, that there's treatment for it," I interject. "So, how often do you have to undergo these treatments?"

"About every three or four months I go in and have it done."

"Is it painful?" I ask sincerely concerned.

"It is a little painful, and I come home sick to my stomach for about a day or two. But I'm not complaining. It's just a small part of my life now, and a small price to pay to live a normal healthy life. I count myself truly blessed."

I home in on the word *blessed* and ask him if he's a Christian.

"Yeah, I am. My family raised me in church."

Now I am even more interested in this guy. He sure has a lot of qualities I like in a man. So, when he asks me if I would like to continue dating him even if he has cancer, I quickly assure him that this wouldn't deter me from seeing him again. I feel a little wall of protection around my heart start to melt as we plan another date.

At this time in my life, Nathan and Melissa were grown and pretty much on their own. I had been single for eight years, and after dating a few men, felt there were few men if any that would ever be marriage material at my age. That is until meeting Kevin.

Kevin and I rode his motorcycle

The next time we went out, Kevin picked me up on his three-wheel motorcycle. I was at a restaurant with my cousin Julie and friend Trish. We took off for the ride and had a really nice day. I enjoyed being with him and listening to the stories about his life. *Such a fascinating man,* I thought. *He's lived such a multi-faceted, interesting life, and yet has such a modest demeanor.* We shared a love for an active outdoor life and a similar sense of humor. Kevin had a playful side and we always had fun together. He also talked about his Christian life. Although I could sense he wasn't as deep in his faith, I was happy that we both shared a Christian life as that was paramount to me. I watched how he treated people with kindness and was the first person to help in a pinch. These things drew me to him.

Kevin had been kind of a small-town baseball hero in his high school days. He had been a winning pitcher all throughout school. He told me about Dia, the girl he had dated all through high school and how he left shortly after graduation to go to a college in Arizona so he could get away from her pestering him to get married.

During one of the final games of his senior year in college, there was a terrible accident. Kevin threw a fast pitch that hit a player in the head. The player had such traumatic brain injury, that it paralyzed him for life. He told me that he had a hard time living with this at first, but that eventually he had forgiven himself and moved on with his life.

Another tragedy was what happened to him when he was in the Air Force after college. He said he let his buddy drive his work truck even though he didn't have a CDL truck license. While they were coming down a hill, his buddy lost control of the truck and plowed into a family: a mom, dad, and their two children. He and his buddy were ejected from the truck, and he watched his buddy die before his eyes.

Kevin was put in the brigade for a while because he broke the law by allowing his friend to drive without a truck license. During the time in jail, he told me, he was sexually abused daily by a gang of men. I found this horrifying and didn't know how he functioned so normally after that much trauma.

One of his assignments took him to Indonesia where he worked on an oil rig out in the ocean. He said the days were hard and grueling, but the days he had off made up for it. He told me about another interesting and dangerous job he had refueling jets in the air. There were a lot more amazing stories he told of his life that captivated me. It caused me to think of him as a very interesting and diverse man. Rarely did I meet someone who had travelled and lived as much of a complex life as I had.

Secure at Last

When he got out of the Air Force, he moved back home to California and landed a very good job. When I met him, he had been working there for many years and was very well established. I grew to love Kevin and his big heart. We dated for about a year and then got married. For the most part, we had a good relationship. We didn't have much time together because of his long commute to work.

However, Kevin and I thoroughly enjoyed our weekends together. We had many friends as well as family get togethers. My kids liked him because he was always a big tease and fun to be around. His humility and kindness drew people to him. We led a small-group Bible Study and attended a great church where I played piano on the worship team. Kevin blended into my family easily, so I felt that I had found a good man and partner for life.

The only hiccup in our relationship was physical intimacy, or the lack of it. Kevin didn't seem to have much of a desire for me in that area. He was polite and caring, and always ready for a big hug and cuddle. I loved curling up next to his big-framed body beside him at night. I loved snuggling and kissing him as we fell asleep. He enjoyed it all as well. But then he'd roll over for a good night sleep.

I attributed that to the fact that he got up and left for work around 4:00 to start his commute. Besides that, I wanted to believe what he told me, that the radiation took away his sex drive. However, nights turned into weeks and months with no sexual intimacy. We had a great friendship, but making love wasn't much a part of our marriage. I began to feel that familiar ache inside that *there must be something wrong with me*. Maybe it was something I was or wasn't doing. I mean, every husband wants to partake whenever they can if their wife is eager, right?

I tried to seduce him. I tried setting the mood with candles, putting on sweet love songs, and wearing sexy nighties. I even met him at the door once with a long brunette wig because he told me that he was more attracted to brunettes than blonds. He looked me up and down, and immediately said, "Now that's a buzz kill." The rejection left me in tears. I felt undesirable, even unfeminine, and unappealing.

It seemed that no matter what I did to try to seduce him, it didn't work. The ache of being turned away hurt deeply. So, after about three years, I decided that I would have to die to that part of our marriage. I pushed the emptiness aside and preoccupied myself with things that weren't painful: creating a home filled with laughter and fun, and meaningful relationships. I reasoned that every other aspect of our marriage was good, so I could let this one part go.

Every three months, Kevin went for his routine radiation appointment. I asked many times to go with him for moral support, but he never wanted me to go. He said he didn't want anyone to see the suffering he went through. Sometimes when he returned home from an appointment, he would be very weak and extremely exhausted. His voice would be raspy because of the radiation. Other times, he would get sick to his stomach and need to go to the bathroom to vomit. A couple of times he fainted in the hallway and had to be carried to the bedroom.

I felt bad for the suffering he had to endure but was thankful it wasn't fatal. Yes, much of our money went to medical bills and back taxes he had incurred, but I totally understood that we had to tackle this together because of his illness.

After we had been married several years, we moved to a somewhat nicer house down the street. Strangely enough, after we moved, I began getting bills in the mail that didn't make any sense to me. I saw that we had paid the moving company $10,000 just to move us a few miles away. I thought, *What in the world? How could this be?* When I questioned Kevin, he said he would look into it.

I began to get statements from credit card companies that we had agreed to get rid of when we first got married. That seemed very odd, so I contested the charges and asked for itemized statements. Sure enough, when I received a copy of the statements, the charges were legitimate. It showed charges for our daily needs, such as groceries, gas, and normal household things that had been purchased in our neighborhood.

I questioned Kevin, and he told me that he was so sorry, but that he was trying to pay off some large chunks of what he owed for medical and back tax bills. He said he had paid a total of $400,000 on these bills. So, he had needed to use credit cards for our everyday needs. He never wanted to share how much he owed on his back bills, so I tried to be understanding, but it was still disconcerting. It felt like some things just weren't adding up. I felt uncomfortable in my spirit. For the first time, I started paying attention to things that didn't make sense to me. I realized there were portions of Kevin's life he didn't share with me. It didn't feel good.

In the past, I had rationalized that he didn't share certain things with me due to his busy job schedule. But with this new information, I began to question anything that seemed strange. One of those was something that had happened a year earlier. His son had accidentally hit a deer and it had totaled his car. For months after that, I received phone calls from the insurance agency asking for Kevin. They became more and more frequent, and they insisted that they needed to talk to him. I relayed this to Kevin several times, and his answer was always, "I'll take care of it."

A couple of weeks later we were having a BBQ with some friends, when the police showed up at the front door with handcuffs to arrest Kevin. I was completely taken by surprise. Not wanting to alarm our friends, I stepped out the front door and closed it behind me. The police told me that Kevin had committed insurance fraud. They said he had lied to the insurance company about the date of his son's accident. He had changed the date to the day after he had reinstated our insurance plan so the car damage would be covered. I had not been aware that our car insurance had lapsed because of lack of payment. Even though he later apologized profusely for his lack of judgment, this didn't set well with me albeit the other issues that weren't adding up.

My mind was reeling with questions. *Why did he lie to me about the insurance company? Why had he not shared with me that he was using credit* *cards to pay thousands of dollars of living expenses from accounts he had supposedly closed? Why was a moving company charging us $10,000 to move down the road five miles? Why wouldn't he let me see the medical or tax bills? Why had he kept everyone from going with him to his radiation appointments? Were all the extra hours he worked really spent at work? He would often tell me that he didn't deserve me, and that if I only knew what he was really like, I wouldn't have chosen him. He had so many outlandish stories about his past. Could some of these be exaggerations or maybe even worse—out and out lies?* I started searching our old bank statements and found large cash amounts taken out with no explanation. There were countless $27 fees. When I asked, he said they were lottery tickets. Later I found out they were bounced-check fees.

The clincher came one day when I learned that there were three different payments for the dating service, match.com. Each payment was for a three-month membership. And then I learned something completely shattering. He was paying for various graphic porn sites. I felt as though someone had just kicked me in the stomach. I was reeling.

Why would he look elsewhere? What about all those lonely nights I had spent lying next to him almost pleading for sex? Why had he rejected me if he actually had a sex drive? The feeling of betrayal was beyond comprehension. The sense of rejection, of not being desirable to my husband had made me doubt my femininity, my worth. I felt I just wasn't enough.

When I saw all the sites he had been on and the crazy money withdrawals, I collapsed inside. *Who is this person I'm married to? What else do I not know about him?* I started to question whether he really had a life-threatening illness. It was like I was living in a dream, or more like a nightmare. I didn't know what was real or unreal anymore. The man that I loved was not the man that I loved!

I was horrified. I was living with someone who had another life. I didn't even know the man I lived with. The final piece of information that pushed me over the edge was discovering that Kevin did not have cancer as he had claimed. I pushed him hard to give me the name of the place he had been receiving his radiation treatments. After several weeks, he finally begrudgingly gave me the name of a clinic. Sure enough, when I checked it out, there was no record of him ever having been there. Just to make sure, I also called every clinic that did that type of treatment in and around our area. I found no record of him ever being at any of them. I can't tell you what a blow that was!

My head and heart ached from this betrayal. I was hurt… crushed…angry. Just imagine finding out that the man you loved and trusted was in reality a completely different person than he portrayed. I felt crazy and unsure of my own judgment in every way. Was I just a pawn that he had preyed on to use as a financial resource for his habits? Had he ever felt ANY real love for me at all? Or was it all a charade? How much of what I believed about him was true? How could he seem so kind on the outside, but be lying and using me at the same time? Of course, I asked him many of these questions and he made up more lies to cover his previous lies.

I wasn't raised in this kind of world at all. This kind of person had never been in my wheelhouse. *Could he change? Would counseling help?* I questioned whether I still loved him, and resolved that I did, and was committed to our marriage. I asked him to move out for a while so we could each get some help.

In those three months, I didn't see any change or progress on Kevin's part. In fact, he lies continued got worse. Once, he called and told me that he had broken his arm and needed $22,000 for surgery. When I asked if I could see him, he replied that it wasn't possible. I found out later that there was no broken arm. He told me that he was living with a friend. When I checked with the friend, I was told he had not stayed there. One night he told me he had taken a bottle of pills to end it all. I tracked down his cell phone with the police. He was in a casino. This happened three times. The third time, the police urged me to move out of my home because they felt he was a psychopath and could be capable of taking me out with himself. For the next few weeks, I lived bouncing around from house to house.

One painful night he called and said that he wanted to come back home. I told him that I loved him and would support him through counseling and whatever else was needed, but that he *had* to be honest with me, otherwise it would never work. I told him that even if he told me that he had killed someone, or if he was gay, or whatever he was covering up, I would be there with him to hold his hand through counseling. But I told him, he had to be honest or there could never be reconciliation or healing.

An hour later, he called me while I was driving to my parents' house for the night. He asked if I would meet him at a certain location, so that he could come clean with the whole truth. Excited and hopeful that he was ready to be honest, I turned the car around and started heading that direction. When I was halfway there, he called again and told me that he just couldn't do it. At that point, I was emotionally weary of living his lies and physically weary from not being able to sleep in my own home. I told him that I needed him to come and take his things out of the house so that I could go back to some sort of normality. There was no talk of divorce, but I was sincerely hoping that with some time apart, he would seek out some much-needed help. I turned around and headed back toward my parents' house.

The next few minutes, a flurry of texts from him ensued, telling me that he wanted to come home. When I suggested that it wasn't a good idea at this time, he began sending scathing texts. I told him that I was on my way to my parents' house to sleep and was going to turn my phone off. But not before seeing this text, "Please come get me before the animals do." He had sent many strange texts like this before, so I ignored it. Just before I turned my phone off, the last text said, "Sherry, you're an f***** coward."

The next morning around 5:00 AM my mom burst into my room holding the phone. She said the police were on the line and had to speak to me. Sleepily I said "Hello," never dreaming of what I was about to hear next. Nobody can ever prepare you for something like this. I was told that Kevin had been found dead; that he had taken his life. It took a couple seconds for the words to sink in. But when they did, I was in horrific, unbelievable shock. I kept screaming, "No, he didn't! No, he didn't!"

I'm not sure how long I screamed and cried and ranted. I was confused and in utter shock. I was unbelievably crushed. It was like such a bad nightmare that it felt it couldn't be true. He was gone? He took his own life? What? It was all so crazy! It couldn't be true!

"Why, oh why, did you have to do that when there could have been so much help for you? There could have been healing," I kept ranting. My mom and dad held me while I reeled from the pain.

Finally, I forced myself to get up and do what had to be done. The first thing was to respond to the police request. They wanted me to come to the station downtown and pick up his belongings. I got dressed and drove like a robot to the station. There was his backpack filled with his phone, computer, and other effects. I filled out some paperwork and then, like a zombie on autopilot, I took his backpack and left to our house. Once inside, it felt surreal to be back inside this place that used to be our happy place; this house where once there had been so much laughter, now felt silently dark and empty. Several people met me there. The first thing I did was to look through his phone and computer for any signs of what had happened. Nothing! It had all been erased. I was frantic to know what had been going on in his mind.

To this day, I don't remember much of the next few days, except that they were filled with immense grief. Kevin and I had agreed that we wanted to be cremated, but some pressed for an open casket. I reached out to a friend who had a mortuary, and they graciously agreed to help prepare him for a viewing.

The day of the viewing came, and a few of his coworkers, family, and friends came to pay their respects. My dad stepped up to the plate to officiate. He asked for those that wanted to honor Kevin with a few words to come forward. A lot of tears were cried as people shared the memories of their relationships with Kevin. Everyone was in shock.

I'm not sure how to even go about explaining the days, weeks, and months that followed. I've never felt as many different feelings from every spectrum flood over me. For a while, I walked around in disbelief and an inability to grasp the finality of things. I just felt numb.

There were many sleepless nights where I tried to gain some semblance of understanding of what he had been thinking. For some reason, it felt very important to understand. What had made him desperate enough to take his life? I tried to figure out why he was so scared to reveal the truth; and what was the truth anyway? I questioned if he had ever loved me at all. Had he ever really had any kind of relationship with God? Who was he really? I could go on and on with the plethora of questions that swirled around endlessly in my head.

Some of the answers to my questions about Kevin came from an unexpected source. I didn't realize that for every suicide case, a detective is assigned to investigate the possibility of a homicide. Officer Ryan was assigned to Kevin. He called to ask me questions many times. I answered as best I could with my limited knowledge. He always showed great sympathy for what I was going through. One day Ryan called and asked if I could meet him at the parking lot of a nearby grocery store.

Officer Ryan got into the passenger seat of my car. He started out by saying that he was deeply sorry for what he was about to reveal. I naively replied, "That's ok, I want to know." He told me that he had been able to unlock Kevin's computer and phone for the three months prior to his death. What he discovered was unnerving.

Apparently, Kevin had a throw away phone; one that you pay for ahead of time. Officer Ryan said that he would use his personal cell phone for an initial contact. Then he would text a reply of "Yes" on his cell phone and call them back from his throw away phone. Ryan revealed some behavior that went on with these phones that I have chosen not to reveal here for specific reasons. I can tell you that after I heard what Kevin's life had really been like, I felt that I had been living in *The Twilight Zone*. I now understood where the large chunks of money withdrawn had gone. I also understood where the many strange deposits had come from.

There is so much more that I could add here, but for discretionary reasons have left out. Because of the way Kevin died, many of the questions I have will never be answered. He took them to the grave with him. Even today, I can only guess at what might be the whole truth. And I've concluded that some things might be better left unknown.

That next year proved to be brutal. I was suffering from PTSD, grief, betrayal, loss, anger, and so many mixed up emotions. I am not proud of how I responded.

I literally shut myself up in my room to be alone and numb my feelings. I didn't want to feel. I didn't want to think or face all the questions churning inside me. It hurt too much. I wanted to sleep, because it was the only time I wasn't tormented by dark thoughts and painful questions and feelings.

To sleep, I employed the use of a very destructive tool, alcohol. I would take a bottle to bed and drink until I slept. If I woke up, I drank some more. I slept full days and nights away. It seemed the only thing I could do to tolerate life. I didn't like myself for it, but at this point I was living in a mixed-up world. What was true, what was a lie? I didn't know, and I didn't know how to cope.

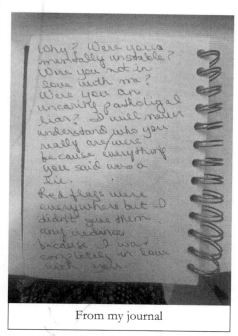

From my journal

My friends and family would call, and I wouldn't answer. I told everyone that I just wanted to be left alone. It seemed like everybody had an opinion. I grew tired of them talking. Nothing helped but drinking and sleeping. No more noise, no more thoughts, just sleep.

My heart was crushed. I was angry, depressed, and confused about everything in my life. *Where was God? Why hadn't he stopped me from marrying this man? Why didn't He show me the truth before I got mixed up in this?* I just wanted to shut everyone out. Even God.

The world didn't make sense anymore. I didn't know what to believe—about myself, or people, or God. All of it was a confusing mess. I seriously didn't know what to make of anything. So, I just crawled under the covers and slept, and slept, and slept. Sometimes I didn't know if it was morning or night.

One day I groggily woke up and a close friend of mine, Jules, was sitting on the duvet next to my bed. She told me she was taking me to our girlfriend Joni's house for a birthday party. I told her to go away and went back to sleep. But she didn't go away. She stayed until I got up that evening, made me get ready and took me to the party. I was still numb and didn't know how to enjoy anything.

Life happened around me and I participated in some of it. But not really. Down in my heart I was distant from everyone and in my own world. There is no road map for how long grief is supposed to last. I kind of lost track of time. Before long, it had been six months. I slowly started caring again and gaining a desire to get better. However, I really wasn't sure how to do that.

Before Kevin died, we had paid in advance for a trip to Hawaii to celebrate our fifth anniversary. The airlines and hotel had said because of the death I could bank the trip for a year. A year later, I took the trip to Hawaii. Alone. Something I had never done before.

When I got there, all I wanted to do was stay in my hotel room and write out my feelings. It helped that I had a beautiful view of the ocean. The ocean had always been my go-to place in hard times. The sound of the waves brought peace and solace to my wounded heart. I sought comfort through prayer and cried a lot. I guess I finally understood that Kevin had a choice, and that his decisions were not God's fault, nor His will. They were made by an individual who for some reason was tortured greatly on the inside.

I knew from the traumas of my own past that I had to forgive what he had done to be free of bitterness. I confessed my unforgiveness to God and asked Him to help me see Kevin like He did. Slowly, my anger turned into sorrow, and I cried for his poor deranged mind and soul. He must have had absolutely no self-worth to have made up fabricated stories about his life. What a sad cry for attention and approval. If he had only known the all-encompassing love that God had for him. I cried for the torment that he had gone through, especially at the end of his life. I let go of the hateful attitudes I had towards him.

I also wrestled with God, asking Him where He was in all of this. No audible voice, no tangible answers to my questions came. But a still soft voice saying that He was there with me, began to break through my hardened heart. He gradually and gently showed me that He had wept with me through the pain. I was not alone in my bed of despondence all those months. These were natural feelings. He had waited for me to feel them all, and to be ready to move on past them. His love had never changed for me. I couldn't receive it through all my blind and angry pain. He had not moved. I had.

He walked me through many of the Psalms that David, the Psalmist had penned. He had been angry, hurt, and betrayed just like I was. He had prayed that God would grind his enemy's teeth to powder. He prayed that God would kill them in merciless ways. Yet, David always came back to God's faithful love that patiently waits for us until we are done ranting. David saw that although he himself was unfaithful, God could and would never be unfaithful. He rejoiced that God always honored His promises.

I think sometimes we try to be our good *Sunday Christian* self when coming to God. If we're feeling angry at others, disappointed with ourselves, resentful towards God, we don't want to talk to Him until we feel we've cleaned up our attitude. We wallow in anger and defeat and try to understand where to go with it.

The BEST place we can go is to the One who loves us completely and utterly unconditionally. He knows what we're thinking and feeling anyway, so why not speak it out? It won't shock Him to hear that we're angry and upset. The best thing we can do is to spill it all out. All those horrible rotten feelings. Scream, cry, vent to Him. It is imperative that we speak our true minds to Him. He can totally handle it. And He's the only One that can come alongside and not only listen but change and heal those attitudes.

You might think: *Who am I to try God's patience? How do I know He's real? How can this be if God is all loving? Where was He when...?* Sometimes we don't feel comfortable voicing these kinds of questions to God. Where does God draw the line on our questioning? However, to ask questions is not the same as disobeying. Refusing to obey is to walk away from God. Asking questions is to go towards God.

Consider someone you have a close relationship with. If you bottle up your questions and negative feelings, how does that effect your relationship? It puts distance between you, right? You can't really feel close to someone if you have hidden feelings and grudges between you and them.

It's the same way with God. If we keep all our questions and disillusionment about Him bottled up inside, we gradually grow distant from Him. We begin to distrust Him, which in turn makes our love for Him grow cold.

We can also be honest with Him about our shortcomings. When we speak the truth to Him about what we feel, whether anger at others, disappointment with ourselves, resentment toward Him the Creator, we open ourselves up to a real relationship; one that can dialogue issues back and forth with a living God. God's presence can be a safe place to reveal our laziness, our grouchiness, and our prideful ways.

God invites transparent confessions about how we pretend to be better than who we really are, how we avoid serving others when we don't feel like it, and how we focus a ton of our energy on getting things: the right shoes, the right car, the right hair style. Confession is important, not because God needs to hear it, but because we need to be willing to express it. When we do so, our conversations with Him become real, open, and honest. Just like in any relationship, this brings us closer with the God Who loves us. It allows Him to answer the deep questions and confessions of our soul. He meets us there with His healing love.

Secure at Last

.

Chapter 18
2013—2015

Walking Toward Healing

As I became honest with God over the next few months and years, He mended the wounds in my heart that I thought were impossible to heal. The wounds of not only what Kevin did to me, but wounds I had created because of my own hurt; the angry questions and bitterness I had towards people and God. Being ruthlessly honest with myself allowed God to work in my heart. Sometimes my questions were answered and sometimes they were just changed to *not having to know*. Simply accepting that God's presence was enough.

One of my questions was: Why do bad things happen to good people? This is an age-old question. I'm sure you've asked it when facing a trauma or difficult situation: a horrific car accident, the death of someone you felt was undeserving, or maybe the painful cancer of someone you love. I think the long and short of it is that we live in a world of sin—a world where we have choices. We often make poor choices in disobedience that affect our world and everyone in it. Then, when negative consequences follow, we blame God. God does not cause evil, the sin in the world has corrupted it. And the effects of sin have a ripple effect that cause us to feel the repercussions.

I've learned that we have a whole different perspective from what God sees. Ours is very limited. Please bear with me for just a few paragraphs as I talk about science and the world we live in. I promise you it has a whole lot to do with some of the questions that we ask.

Our bodies are not eternal, so we can only see this finite timeline that we're living in. God created our timeline to be linear, with a past, present, and future. But He Himself is outside of that timeline. He always has been. He didn't have a beginning. And He doesn't have an end. That's what eternity means. It goes on and on and on with no end. That's hard for us to understand because it's not like that in our four-dimensional world.

In this life and mortal body, we live in the four dimensions of height, width, depth, and time. That's it. However, scientists have proven that there are at least 10 dimensions, and some say even more than that. We can't see, feel, or experience the other dimensions because our senses are limited to the four we live in. Whether or not we can sense them, they are all around us. That's a fact. It helps to have a picture to understand it, so here you go.

If you and I were only two-dimensional beings—height and width—like a stick figure on a computer screen, and something that is in three dimensions (depth) put its finger on the computer screen, we would probably not believe it was there because we couldn't sense it. However, it really was there, just outside of our limited senses of height and width.

168

That's how it is with God. He lives outside of our four dimensions, so sometimes we may not understand Him and His ways. I think a lot of our questions come from our blind perspective. If we can't understand God, we think there's something wrong with Him or that He doesn't exist. No. We just don't have the whole picture yet. It's odd how we humans want to understand everything about God, when if we could, He wouldn't be God – quite *other* than us. We have questions that might never get answered this side of eternity. I must be ok with that now. The Bible says that we see through a distorted glass right now. But when we see God face-to-face, it will be clear and undistorted because we'll be in His dimensions. I can't wait. And I have a lot of questions stored up for Him.

I wish I could say that when I came home from Hawaii my heart was completely healed. The truth is that sometimes deep wounds like this take time. I had to choose new ways of coping and dealing with the pain. Drinking and sleeping the days and nights away was not going to help me heal. I had to choose new coping skills. One of those was finding something to give me purpose.

I've always loved decorating and redoing homes. A couple of my friends' homes were in a gated golf community in the Foothills. They asked me to help them with redecorating. I threw myself into upgrading their décor. I absolutely loved it. I found out that I could lose myself for hours on end while making a home beautiful. For one thing, it was a physical activity, which was a good outlet for my angst. For another, when I saw the result, I received a tremendous amount of satisfaction.

A few months after these homes were completed, I received a surprise phone call from a woman who managed a large real estate company. She asked if I would consider coming to work staging homes for her open houses. I was honored but told her that I didn't have a degree in design.

Staging by Sher

My business card

She told me that she had seen the houses I had redecorated and was willing to take a chance on me. I was elated. It would be a perfect opportunity to do something I loved as well as get paid for it. I accepted her offer and began working for her.

The job required quite a bit of time and a lot of physical labor, but I loved it. A real estate agent would give me the address of a home he or she was listing in an Open House. I'd go to the home and take pictures of every room. Then, I would design colors and styles that suited that home. The company had a huge warehouse full of various styles of furniture and decor. I chose and tagged all the furniture and decor I wanted to use, and it was delivered the next day. Then, the physical labor started of placing the furniture and decor inside the home. The hope was that in two or three days, the house would have been transformed into a beautiful model home that would capture a greater price for the seller.

I often worked 12–15-hour-days to accomplish it. Imagine moving into a home and designing it in three short days; pictures, rugs, furniture, linens, towels, dishes – everything needed to be ready and beautiful. There was a lot of physical labor involved. Perfect for healing a broken-hearted person who had been sleeping her days away. I thank God for bringing me to that job at the right time. It consumed my time, energy, and thoughts, so that there was no strength left for dwelling on Kevin's death.

In looking back, many of the things involved in doing this job benefited my emotional wellbeing as well. I do want to point out that before I could receive these benefits, I had to be ready and open to healing. That is the first step; **being ready**. At this point, after spending six months in bed, I was ready to take the journey towards healing.

The second step was **getting physical exercise**, which I gleaned through starting the new job. If you are hurting, stressed or angry, physical exercise is one of the best pick-me-ups you can do. It releases tension, gives you endorphins (those happy hormones in your brain), and because your sleep is enhanced, you also boost your serotonin (another happy hormone). Sometimes the last thing you want to do is make your body move. I encourage you to just do it anyway. Your choice of exercise may be completely different from someone else's. Whatever it is, get up and do it. I'm serious. I assure you it will help.

The third step was *doing something that I thoroughly enjoyed.* The satisfaction of accomplishing something and doing a good job, helps with self-esteem. We are each gifted with our own unique talents that bring us fulfillment. Maybe you're great with plants and love gardening. Why not throw yourself into making or enhancing your yard or even a community garden project?

My dear friend, Chrissy, went through an emotional crisis a couple years ago. They had just moved into a house with almost an acre of dirt in the backyard — a blank slate waiting to be designed. She threw herself into creating the backyard of her dreams. Again, a lot of physical labor and doing something she loved. The process of the design and the fruit of her labor slowly brought her back to a sense of wellbeing. Ask yourself what it is that *you* love doing. What are *you* good at doing? Take some time to plan, then pour yourself into it. The process and the result can be very healing.

The fourth step that helped me heal was *journaling and keeping short accounts.* This also aided in processing and facilitating my growth. I encourage you to dive in and write. Even if it's just a sentence or paragraph. Writing helps you see what works and what doesn't in facilitating your improvement. In the morning I would write down my emotional state, and then look at what I could do to keep myself from spiraling downward. I'd ask God to give me His thoughts when my mind would go on its own ranting rampage or when memories surfaced. I would choose to think about positive things instead.

At the end of my day, I tried to journal what my triggers had been and what had helped keep me from spiraling downward into anger and depression. This way I could be somewhat in control of my healing instead of letting my mind and emotions control me.

The fifth step was learning to **change my self-talk** and the way I viewed my situation. I asked myself questions like: *What kind of person do I want to be? What character traits do I want to see in myself?* Then, I created 3x5 cards with sentences that proclaimed that I was that person. The visual helped immensely. Most of who we are is determined in our head; what we say when we talk to ourself. In fact, there's a great book by that title. *What to Say When You Talk to Yourself*, by Shad Helmstetter.

Since we were young, we've all been measuring our circumstances as they happened. How we perceived ourselves in these situations became our reality. Of course, all of us have been treated unfairly at times, and have believed lies about ourselves because of it. This has created a mental image of who we think we are, whether true or untrue. We react and respond to the world through this lens. It doesn't matter if what we think about ourselves is true or false. Our core beliefs are based on how we viewed ourselves in these situations or life events. We travel down life's road with this sense of who we are.

Here's a real-life example: A few years ago, I went to a Girlfriends Group (yes, that's actually what we called it). This group had been started by my friend Connie who lives in my neighborhood. There were about 20 ladies and they had been meeting once a month for about four years. I went along with Connie, excited to form some new friendships with women living around me.

The format was a casual dinner and games at someone's home. As the evening progressed, I began feeling like the odd man out. My normal talkative self grew quiet as I processed that old familiar feeling of rejection. My old self-talk began in my head. *Everybody else is interesting and engaging, but you are not. You're different.* I felt that old familiar, gut-wrenching pain in the stomach that I had experienced as a child. There it was! That old familiar button. All I wanted to do was escape and get out of there. I'm not sure I even said goodbye to anyone as I left earlier than anyone else.

Looking back, I can see that it was all in my head. Because I believed that people were ignoring me and that I was different, I interpreted every action as rejection. When talking with Connie about it later, she said that this couldn't have been farther from the truth. I missed out on a lot of fun and new relationships that night because of an inaccurate view of myself as well as negative self-talk.

You too probably have buttons that get pushed by situations. Sometimes you can even see that your reaction is irrational, and yet it persists. This is because our brain is like a computer hard drive. It doesn't decipher if something is truth or fiction. It just records and regurgitates what we tell it. The more years we have fed it negative data, the more it is ingrained in our self-talk. How can we change the data, and hence our self-talk?

We can begin to feed our brain new data and information. Tell it the truth about ourselves and/or what we want to be true about ourselves. It sounds crazy but it works. It takes time, but it works. Let's take my recent situation for example. My negative talk was that something was wrong with me causing people not to accept me. What is the truth about me? I am a loving and kind person who has a lot of interesting life experiences to bring to the table. I am a good listener and have a quick wit. God has given me the gift of encouragement and discernment. Now, lest this seem braggadocios, please know that I truly don't see myself as better than anyone else. Anyone. Honestly! We all have great value. You and I included. God created me with my uniqueness just as He create you with yours.

After returning from Hawaii, I worked to change my negative self-talk and instead began speaking out loud the strengths that God had given me. Don't worry, I was alone when I did it. I found that writing them out on 3x5 cards helped as well. I placed the cards in places where I could see them every day: on my car dashboard, my bathroom mirror, and my laptop computer. It's not necessary always to say them aloud, but there is a benefit for our brain to receive them through as many senses as possible.

Remember, the brain doesn't know if it's true or false, it just records the information. The longer we have said these negative things to ourselves, the longer it takes to replace them with the positive.

Eventually the brain begins to play the new tape in our minds and the thoughts become our new self-identity. And the new thoughts bring new behavior.

It almost sounds too simple to be true. But it IS true. The next time you get offended or angry, ask yourself what negative self-talk was involved. Did the offense trigger a lie that you believe about yourself? When did that lie start? What was happening in your life when you started believing that lie? Go back and search deep in your heart. When you recover these memories, ask Jesus to go through the events with you. Picture Him holding your hand and lovingly comforting you. I'm not asking you to believe a lie. The truth is that Jesus *was* there with you when those hurtful events happened: when big people treated you badly, and when you started to believe lies about yourself. He cared greatly that you were hurt.

Most of these hurts happened when we were forming our early opinions about who we were. Ask Him to show you the truth about who you really are or about who you want to become. Speak these truths over your life. Start new self-talk. Whenever you start telling yourself the old lies, replace them with the truth.

The sixth thing that helped was going on **medication**. During those first six months after Kevin's death, my whole body shook uncontrollably. I also had a hard time putting words together into full sentences. My thoughts were jumbled, and it was hard for me to follow through on a complete thought. I often began to speak and midway through would forget what I was talking about.

I also started suffering from panic attacks. I can only describe them as overwhelming emotional and physical senses of impending doom. Physically, everything inside you starts racing and your chest feels like it's being pounded by a heavy weight. A friend suggested that I go to a holistic hormone doctor (one who practices naturopathic medicine). My chemistry and adrenaline had been severely affected by all of the emotional trauma. The doctor prescribed some hormone creams that helped greatly.

I also started taking anti-anxiety anti-depressants to help the tremors and panic attacks. In time, these medications helped to relax my body so that I could heal. It also helped me to sleep deep and get the rest that my body and emotions so desperately needed. There should be no stigma for medication. It may be precisely what our body is missing and can help bring us back to health.

So, if I could put in a nutshell the things that helped bring about the healing process:

1. Be ready to take action in order to be healed.
2. Get physical exercise regularly.
3. Start doing something you thoroughly enjoy.
4. Journal.
5. Change your self-talk.
6. Practice medication (prayer).

Secure at Last

Chapter 19
2015—2022

My Life Is Amazing

—

Knock on Wood

Answering the phone, I hear a somewhat familiar voice on the other end. "Hey Sherry, this is Jay Francis."

Remembering a couple of great conversations on the phone with this man, I perk up, "Hey Jay! It's good to hear from you again. How have you been?"

"Well, I wanted to let you know that I'll be coming to your town next week and wondered if you'd like to meet up for dinner one night?"

My heart is smiling as I answer quickly, "I would love that!" From our past conversations, I know that this man is a strong Christian and seems to have a fantastic personality and sense of humor, he's outdoorsy, and loves family like I do.

Hmmm, I think as I drive to the restaurant the next week. *This is a quality guy. Wonder what he's like in person.*

Walking towards the door, I see Jay and recognize him from his pictures. That's a good first sign right there, as most pictures of people online are about ten years old. He stands about 5'10', dark hair, and a huge warm smile and kind eyes. His hug feels good, and I know that I already feel comfortable with him.

After four hours of engaging conversation, the waitress comes over for the third time and with a smile on her face says, "You two! I wish I could have sat in on your conversation tonight. It looked really fun. If it was up to me, you could stay all night, but my manager sent me over to tell you that we really do have to lock the doors now. The staff are all going home."

We both laugh and apologize as Jay walks me outside to my car. "I thoroughly enjoyed this evening, Sherry. Do you think you might have another free night this week while I'm in town?"

"Let's do it! How about Friday? I have to go up to Placerville to pick up a piano from a church. If you wouldn't mind helping me transport it in your truck, that would be awesome."

"Absolutely! I'd love to help. It's a date."

And off we go our separate ways. All the way home, my mind is churning, *What a great evening. It feels like I've known Jay forever. If only he didn't live 4 hours away. I mean that's a little far to date somebody. Oh well, at least I know we'll be good friends.*

Secure at Last

Friday is here and I find myself a little more excited to see Jay than I anticipated. On the one-hour drive to pick up the piano, he and I just pick right back up where we left off at the restaurant. Not only is the visit with Jay great, but I love the piano. While I'm enthusiastically trying out the different bells and whistles it has, my brother Rick calls. It's bad news.

"Hey, Bear" (his pet name for me) "Mom had a bad fall in her driveway about an hour ago, and she's in an ambulance on her way to Auburn Hospital."

My heart squeezes tight with worry as our mom is 80 years old. "Oh no, Bubba!! How bad is she?" I choke.

"They think she's probably broken her hip."

"Oh man! I'm up in Placerville without my own car. I'll race home right now, pick up my car and meet you up there! I'll be there as fast as I can." I say as I hang up the phone quickly.

Jay lightly puts his hand on my back for reassurance and tells me he'd be glad to take me to the hospital. "I know exactly where Auburn Hospital is. That's where my grandson was born," he says.

Jay quickly packs the truck with the new piano, and we take off in a hurry.

Arriving there, I quickly introduce Jay to my dad, brother, and the friends and congregation members of my folks' church who have gathered in the lobby. "Jay, do you mind if I leave you here and go in to visit my mom?"

"Of course not" he assures me; again placing his arm gently on my back. "Stay in there as long as you need to. I'll be praying along with the rest of the folks out here!" Something about Jay calms my spirit and I feel my body relax a bit.

When I finally walked out from my mom's room, it had been a full three hours, and I was worried that Jay would be a little perturbed.

Instead, I found him easily chatting with the group of people huddled in the waiting room. *Wow! What a good-hearted person this man is. Not only did he stay but he also prayed with the people who were worried about my mom.* I was impressed.

It was after midnight by the time Jay dropped me off at my doorstep. "You can't make that 3 1/2-hour drive home this late." I told him. "Why don't you stay here in my brother's room? He's not here tonight." My brother Rick had been staying with me for a few months while he was preparing to relocate his family.

"Well, if you don't think it's an imposition, that would be a lot easier." Jay looked genuinely thankful for the offer.

The next morning, I came into the living room clad with my long bathrobe, hair tousled, and bare faced. Jay met me with a fresh cup of coffee that he had just brewed. I was impressed by his thoughtfulness. We sat on the couch and talked like old friends, hour-after-hour, until early afternoon. It was almost like someone sprinkled fairy dust on both of us. At one point, we looked at each other and said something like, "I feel like I've come home to my soul mate." Ok, before you gag on this crazy statement, let me say that neither one of us would recommend telling someone that you might be falling in love a week after you meet them. Somehow it worked for us.

We realized quickly that we had come through very similar experiences and challenges. I had never dated a man who was such a giver, and it was like water to my thirsty soul. We shared a love for God and for people.

Four weeks into our dating, we invited our daughters and their husbands and kids to spend Easter together with us. It ended up being rather awkward. We were, in fact, asking our girls to see us as a couple after only four short weeks. And let's just say they didn't share our enthusiasm. There were a lot of general pleasantries exchanged and a lot of awkward silent moments. At one point I took Jay's daughter Katie into my bedroom and told her that I was not playing with her dad's heart, and that she could trust that I truly saw a future with him. She just looked at me with a look of, "Yeah, whatever, crazy lady."

The one detail that complicated our relationship was the distance. He lived in a small mountain community about four hours away from the city where I lived. That made getting to know each other a little challenging, but we made it work. Many times, Jay drove down just for the day and turned around to drive the distance back in the middle of the night so he could get to work the next morning. We craved time together and knew that one of us was going to have to make a move closer to the other.

Around the same time I met Jay, I was also able to buy a house. It was the first time that I had ever lived alone, and the solitude provided a place of peace and healing. The home was small but had good bones. I could imagine the upgrades needed to make it beautiful and decided this was a great project to pour my energy into. It's interesting to look back and see how working on this house was a tangible parallel to working on myself.

I started by taking down the wall that separated the kitchen from the living room. If you've never put a hammer through a wall and hacked it down, you're missing a truly satisfying adrenaline rush. Or maybe I just needed to pound on something. In any case, it sure felt good. I continued to work on the projects that I could handle and hired subcontractors to do the things I couldn't. When finished, the kitchen was completely gutted and updated, new flooring was put in throughout the house. The master bathroom was also gutted, and redone, new updated windows were installed throughout, and the house was painted inside and out. The backyard was completely landscaped with a large concrete patio to facilitate BBQ's and outdoor time.

The entire project took a year and was healing for my body and soul. I think I was trying to make this run-down house into a brand new and beautiful home, just as I wanted to be *reborn*. As the house started changing, I could see things changing inside of me as well.

Wedding Day with Jay

Ten months after meeting Jay, we were happily engaged to be married and asking God to show us where we should live after marriage. Jay had been wanting to live closer to his daughter Katie, and son-in-law Luke and grandchildren for years. That was not far from my home. We asked God for a sign. If He wanted us to live in my area, we asked Him to open a job for Jay there. My family was spending Thanksgiving in the mountains near Jay when we got a call from a company in my area that wanted to hire him. His position would be identical to his current job, and the location was right between our two daughters' homes. We both rejoiced. For many years, my heart had desired to provide a loving home to host activities for family and friends.

After Jay began his job near me, God opened a beautiful home in a small golf community located near four lakes and a river. We got married and began enjoying life together. It nearly took my breath away to realize how God had begun to fulfill every one of my desires.

For the last six years, we have enjoyed hosting family events, watching our eight grandchildren grow up, leading small group Bible Studies for our church, and living life with old and new friends. These have been the best years of my life, fulfilling dreams that had lain dormant for years. We have had a marriage full of giving and loving on both sides. Our children are all married to people we ourselves would have hand-picked for them. And of course, there is no love like a grandparent's love. We have been thrilled to enjoy, as well as influence, our grandchildren, whom we adore. We have been blessed in every way and could not be more thankful! Yet we had no way of knowing a huge challenge lay just ahead....

A recent extended family gathering

Christmas with our grands

Another recent extended family gathering,
That's Rusty on the far left next to Jay.

Chapter 20
2021—2022

Big Challenges Can Lead to Big Miracles

Outside the hospital, Jay rolls the passenger seat back in his truck. He carefully lifts me out of the wheelchair and into the truck's cab. The reality of how broken my body is suddenly becomes more real as I am out of the hospital and back in the real world. Traveling down the road, I let out yelps and screams. "Oohhhhh, go slower," I groan, as each bump sends searing pain throughout my body.

The hospital staff has sent us home with a pain prescription for oxycodone, a drug that I am told will soon be my best friend. "Hang on, Baby. We're going to get you some pain meds soon. We just need to find a Walgreens that's open at this time of night," Jay says trying to comfort me.

His voice seems so loud. And it is then that I realize that every sound seems to be amplified through my body like a wave, intensifying the pain. My mind reels. *I don't think either one of us anticipated the gravity of what I would be experiencing once I was unhooked from the hospital IVs. Maybe we should have listened to the doctor's warning. He had said it was too soon to leave the hospital. But it's too late. Now I'm on my way down this uncharted territory. I'm scared!*

The car ride to Walgreens seems to last for hours. When we finally get there, Jay hops out of the car and his last words to me are, "I'll be right back, Honey." Picturing a ten-minute wait, I nod my head. My pain medicine is wearing off quickly. Ten minutes pass, then another ten, and then another. My painful body is carefully squirming in my seat trying every way possible to get the weight off my pelvis. I was told that I crushed it on all four sides; sitting on it is excruciating. Standing up is impossible. I begin to cry out of desperation as yet another ten minutes rolls on by.

Why, oh, why, did I leave the hospital bed? What was I thinking? Where is Jay? Oh, please, God, just help me find a comfortable position. I can't do this anymore. My thoughts are becoming frantic. I scream at God "Why did you save me? Why didn't you just bring me home to heaven to be with You? I don't want to be here." Finally, after working myself into hysterics, Jay opens the car door. It's been over an hour.

Jay explains to me, "Honey I'm so sorry! There were problems with the Insurance Company. Here I've got some water in the back. Let's get this medicine in you right now." I am grateful for Jay's devotion to helping me get out of this pain. When we arrive home, he carries me over and onto the couch, which fortunately reclines similarly to the hospital bed. The pain meds start kicking in and I find myself falling fast asleep.

The next morning, I wake up with a beautiful flower garden all around me. "This is crazy! Where did all these dozens of flowers come from Babe?" I ask Jay overwhelmed with emotion. "I didn't even notice them last night."

"Oh Honey, you are loved! There have been dozens of people coming over the last few days. They've been very concerned about you and have offered to help in any way they can."

Jay and I start to read the many cards that accompany these treasures with tears flowing down our faces. What love our friends and neighbors have poured out so graciously. My heart is humbled and touched by their caring generosity. *It's only been five days since my life was turned upside down, but somehow it seems like I've been alone for weeks,* I think. These beautiful acts of kindness are like warm arms reaching out to touch and hold me in my brokenness. And suddenly I don't feel alone anymore. It truly does take a village.

My hubby tried to get me to stand up just about once every hour. He had been instructed by the physical therapist at the hospital to have me walk to keep my muscles from atrophying. We learned later that this was the worst thing I could have done, considering I had crushed my pelvis, leaving no foundation connecting my lower half with my upper half. Being the dutiful husband that he is, Jay got me up to walk with my walker once each hour like he had been instructed. We soon realized that as soon as I tried to put any pressure on my feet, my pelvis would give way and start making popping sounds. There was nothing supporting my pelvis, so it wiggled and popped until I sat back down again. This might sound crazy, but the pain felt like I was trying to push a baby out of my pelvis. It was so intense, I screamed out loud and cried uncontrollably.

The second night was possibly the worst night of pain since the accident. Jay was very cautious about how many pain pills to give me. I found out later that someone he loved had gotten addicted to this kind of medication, so he was trying to prevent that from happening to me. That night, the pain was at a ten for literally hours. Some have said that a *ten* on the 0–10 pain scale means that if there were a gun nearby, you would shoot yourself. I lost it and went into uncontrollable sobs. You know the kind of ugly cry that has you doubled over gasping for your next breath?

Jay contemplated taking me back to the hospital but decided first to call our nurse friend Stephanie who lived down the street. When she heard me screaming in the background, she asked Jay how much medication I was taking. He told her that he was being very conservative. I could hear her lecture him emphatically, "Give her as much medication as it takes to bring the pain level down to being manageable. And if you can turn on some soft background music and gently rub her back, that might help calm her down." She explained to him that once the pain level was up to a ten, it was very hard to get it back down. She assured him that it was fine to medicate me until I was comfortable, even if it took more than the recommended dose. I will be eternally grateful for nurse Stephanie. Because of her wisdom and advice, I never experienced that intensity of pain again.

Jay and I were both baffled at many aspects of the accident. During my few waking hours, we would go over the events trying to figure out what led to the accident, and how I could have flown through the sunroof, landing 45 feet from the road, and not have been killed. The ambulance and first responders as well as those who had seen the accident, thought a body bag was needed. They reported that nobody could have survived that accident. The wrecking yard owner also told Jay that by the looks of the car, he couldn't believe I was alive.

I must admit that there were moments at the beginning where I wished that I *had* died in the accident. I didn't want to be here on earth. When Jay was gone on an errand one day, I vented my anger to God. "Why did You make me come back here? I was so close to being with You in Heaven. And now I'm in a broken body full of pain, full of shame, and defeat. Why didn't You let me go be with You?" I screamed from my wheelchair. I calmed down later and apologized to God for my prideful anger. But, for a few weeks, I resented that I had to remain on earth.

I've always had an eager appetite to read books on Heaven and after-death experiences. Figuring that if this life is just a few short years and the afterlife is endless, shouldn't I find out as much as possible about it?

Death doesn't scare me because I've been faced with it twice and have been with close friends when they have left their body for the afterlife. In fact, when friends have died, I've been a little jealous that they were able to shed these limited dimensional bodies and trade them in for perfect heavenly bodies. I've always looked at life this way. They've gone on the best vacation before me, and I will get to join them later. It's not a morbid death-wish, but a Christmas morning childlike excitement for the exhilarating life to come. I believe we're all going to be surprised at the great magnitude of what God has planned for us.

Through these months on the road to recovery I finally realized that God must not be finished with His work for me down here on earth. There is always a bigger picture in His plan than what we can see from our current vantage point. My aim is to accomplish all that He has for me to do while I'm still here. I look for His purposes daily.

A few days after the accident, we received a police report. "Honey, this report doesn't look good for you at all. The witnesses are saying that you randomly made an illegal left turn into the middle of oncoming traffic. People are wondering if you were trying to commit suicide. The policeman that attended to you at the scene said that he asked you that question a few times."

"Of course not, that's ridiculous. Why would I want to commit suicide? I know that's not what happened. Dang, I just wish I could remember more of the details," I moaned. All I could remember was a flash image of my doggie Chloe and me leaning to the left side of the car. And that was it. That was the only semblance of recollection I had of the accident.

Chloe had been my constant companion for 15 years. She was half chihuahua and half mini pincher. She had these uncanny human-looking eyes that peered at you as if she understood every word being said. Chloe was the one I cuddled with under the covers after

190

Kevin died. My daughter had given her to me to give me company after she had married Travis. My little Chloe went with me almost everywhere, my constant shadow. I loved her to pieces.

The night of the accident, she had jumped in the car with me as usual. Chloe loved going on car trips and liked to stand next to the driver's seat on the middle console while we drove. Because of her age, she had just started jumping onto my lap whenever we got onto the main highway outside of our gate. As usual that night, she jumped onto my lap. I wrestled between putting on my seat belt and handling her. Sadly, the seat belt never got fastened. After the impact, I flew through the sunroof and landed about 45 feet away in a barbed wire fence. Not a good situation no matter how you look at it.

A couple of days after the police report arrived, Jay was scrolling through Facebook. "WHAT??? Oh my gosh, Honey, they're talking about your accident here on Facebook!" Jay yelled, as he pointed to his laptop. "This is a random Facebook Group I'm on because of work. It's mostly for firemen and policemen in this area, but I'm on it because of all the acres of our work property. Listen, it's talking about an accident the night of November 25th, and it's saying they didn't think the driver of the red Lexus made it out alive. That's you, Babe, they're talking about you."

Neither one of us were prepared for what he saw next. Someone had posted a video of my accident taken from their car dash-cam. We looked at each other in amazement and screamed the same thing, "Oh my gosh...." Jay quickly cast the video onto our TV screen. Here it was. The missing information in my memory of what had caused the accident. We watched in horror as my car veered off the road slightly onto the right shoulder. A cloud of dust plumed out behind the car as I drove. Then, in an instant the car made a quick left into the oncoming traffic. We watched it again and again, freezing each frame to recap every detail of what had happened.

After analyzing it, we put the pieces together and had a good picture of what had happened that night. Some distraction had caused me to veer over to the left shoulder. Knowing from experience, that this was the spot where Chloe always jumped in my lap, we decided this was a strong possibility. Most likely I looked up from my lap and saw that the road was making a sharp left. The video showed that I over-corrected to make the curve from the right shoulder of the road, causing me to cross over the line into oncoming traffic. "Honey, can you believe this? We would never have been able to prove that you didn't make a turn into traffic on purpose. But here on the video it shows the reason you did it. The highway had a slight left turn, and you were over-correcting from the right side of the road. This is a crazy miracle to show us clearly what happened. Isn't it amazing that a man had a dash-cam on at exactly your location when the accident happened? And that he would even post it here on an obscure site in another county that I just so happen to be a member of. Can you see what an unbelievable set of happen stances this is?" We stopped right there and thanked God for this unexpected gift. It was clear that I caused the accident, but also that it was not intentional as it seemed to the onlookers.

The next few days were somewhat melded together in my memory. Pain medication has a way of doing that to a person. As I recall, I slept most of the first few days. By the second week, we started to fall into a routine of sorts. Jay was able to take some time off from work. To say that he was kind and attentive throughout my recovery is an understatement. He was literally an angel of mercy, taking care of every need that I had.

I couldn't do anything for myself, which sometimes frustrated me to no end. I felt uncomfortable asking him for help, so he watched me closely and responded to my spoken as well as unspoken requests. Never once did he complain; and I mean never. He saw me at my very worst, physically, and emotionally, and still loved me. I am eternally grateful to God for my man!

At my first doctor's visit, the doctor reiterated that walking was the last thing I should be doing. He explained that for my pelvis to heal, it was imperative not to move off the couch for at least two months. For potty needs, I should use the porta-potty next to the couch. Staying still wasn't going to be a problem, as the pain kept me immobile and ready to comply.

A typical day during this time of recovery began with my hubby cheerfully greeting me as I woke up from a semi-reclined position on the couch. "Good morning, beautiful." Next, he filled my drink bottle and gave me the seemingly endless supply of daily prescription pills. Next followed the shot of blood thinner into my abdomen. "What do you feel like eating today?" He coaxed, as my appetite was almost nonexistent. Jay became an expert at making oatmeal, as that was one of the few things that sounded appetizing to me; and it's a good thing because it was one of the few things he knew how to cook!

After breakfast, Jay would lift me into the wheelchair so I could wheel myself to the back of the house. It was there at my vanity, which held my Bible and journal, that I found peace and purpose for living each morning. This became my *God-spot*. For some reason this room became my favorite room to meet with Jesus. It was quiet, private, and had a great view of the backyard. It became a place I visited often throughout the day. Of course, God could have met me in any room. But for some reason, it became a familiar oasis where my heart would be touched, comforted, and molded. A place where Jesus' presence would permeate my soul. There had been years that I had struggled to consistently keep a devotional time. But now, I found that my whole being longed for it. My soul was thirsty and the only thing that quenched it was God's presence. It was the one place I felt connected and whole, strengthened, and healed.

The Bible became increasingly illuminated and clearer to me than it ever had been. You know when you're reading a really good book and you just don't want to put it down? That's how it was with the books in the Bible. I started in Matthew and continued reading through the New Testament, with a desire for more understanding. It was like I was in a bubble with God. His truths were delivered perfectly through a quiet voice that spoke to me throughout the day. I didn't have to search for Him. He was right there constantly with me. And His presence was changing my perspective on life.

I could see clearly that the temporal things I had held close before were not as important as they had been. I had always desired a nice comfortable home and had spent many hours decorating and rearranging it to make it picture perfect. Now, this felt so insignificant. I felt I had come from death to life. God had literally protected me as I went through the sunroof and kept me here on this earth. And I was pretty sure that His reason wasn't so that my house would be perfectly decorated; or my body would stay young and healthy; or Jay and I would have the perfect social life. These things had preoccupied my life before the accident. Now, they seemed trivial. What would last and go on into eternity with me after I died? Only eternal things. My relationship with God and other people.

This daily communion with God filled me up completely. I found myself content with no desire to search outside myself for things that would fulfill. There was no need for it. God satisfied my heart completely. Even the desire to please people and to have their approval faded. That childhood button of belonging, of fitting in with others, was completely satisfied.

Sometime in week two, Jay had a sobering conversation with me. "Sherry, you know this is going to be a huge hit that will impact our future, right? I mean, this changes everything for us. Financially, we won't be able to retire as early as we would have. And physically, we won't be able to do a lot of the things we enjoyed doing in the past. We won't be able to pay the house off and get a motor home for travel like we were planning. Our lives are going to be affected by this for a very long time, if not forever. We're both going to have to tighten our spending belt for a long while."

Jay was breaking down the already bad news to an even more graphic long-term perspective. It had been two weeks, and he had been holding it together and taking care of my needs, working from home, as well as taking care of what I usually did around the house. We were seeing the medical bills pile up, and he wasn't sure if or when I would ever recover. I think he just needed to vent, but it was a little too much weight for me to carry at that moment, so I just nodded with a "God will take care of us, Honey," response.

As hard as things were at the time, Jay and I were overwhelmed with the love and compassion poured out on us from our family, neighbors, and friends. My longtime friend, Jules, and next-door neighbor friend, Michelle, organized a meal train that lasted all through the holidays and throughout January. Although I had very little appetite, what a blessing it was for Jay to be able to come home from work and sit down to a homecooked meal complete with dessert. I found a new love for chocolate and started looking forward to our delectable dessert each night.

Visits from my family and friends did a lot to buoy my spirit. Usually every day, there was at least one person popping in for a visit. My mom and daughter were the first to come. I'll never forget seeing them for the first time. It had been just a few short days before, when they had spent Thanksgiving Day together wondering if I was going to live or not. Now, here I was home and alive, albeit a pretty banged up mess. When we saw each other for the first time, we all burst into tears. Nothing makes you appreciate your family more than a near-miss at death.

Melissa visiting me for my birthday, on day twenty-two after the accident

Secure at Last

Different members of my family took turns caring for me. Mostly Mom, Melissa, and Cousin Julie. It did my spirit good to be with those I loved, even though I wore out quickly and slept a fair amount. They exhibited their love in so many tangible ways. They wheeled me into the bathroom and lifted me onto the commode. They filled my beverage bottle, kept track of my medications, and gently encouraged me when I was down. I will forever be grateful. There are few people I connect with better than my brother, Rick. I remember the first day he popped in for a *chin wag*. I had been home for three weeks. "Hey, Bear," he called out with a big smile on his face. "You look great." Of course, I knew this was a big fat lie! I was fully aware of how badly swollen, black and blue, and cut up my road-rash-face looked. But he's always had a way of smooth-talking the ladies. I smiled as it pleasantly worked for me that day. He sat down on the couch and took me in his arms. Soon, we both had tears streaming down our faces, as we realized afresh how close I had come to leaving this earth.

"Hey, Bear, do you realize how important it was that the vehicle your car hit matched yours so perfectly?"

"What? I don't get it." I knew Rick's opinion on mechanics could be trusted because of his degree in the field.

"Well, the SUV you hit had a bumper that was exactly the same height as your SUV. If it had been a smaller car with a lower bumper, it most likely would have lifted you up and flipped you over a few times. If it had been a bigger car with a higher bumper, it would have gone right through the car and into your body. Bear, if you had to hit a car, this was the best kind to hit, as your bumpers matched perfectly. This is just one more piece of evidence that it's a miracle you're alive," he tearfully explained.

As I mentioned earlier, journaling has long been an integral part of my life. Here are a few excerpts from my journal dated in early December:

***Mom stayed with me today so Jay could go to work. She is such a giver and amazes me with her unselfish love and care. She is 85, so of course she can't do

196

things as fast or as well as she used to do. Watching her clean the house today made me smile because it looked like it was so hard for her to do, and yet she pushed through and did it anyway. Why? Because she loves me and wants things to be the best they can for me. Just like I still want to do for my daughter Melissa and my son Nathan. And just like Melissa wants to do for her daughter Ella and her sons Brooklyn and Jude. We all love our babies and each one has their own special place in our heart no matter how old they are. I am still my mama's baby. And Nate and Melissa are still mine.

Father God, help me not to take my mom for granted. Help me remember to show her how grateful I am for all she does in my life. I'm amazed at all the sacrifices she's made. I want to show her how valuable she is to me, even though age is affecting her abilities. Someday she won't be here, and I'll never hear her voice again. I need to make it a priority to spend time with her and show her how much she's valued.

***My son and his fiancé, Melissa, came up from Southern California on one of the hardest days of this journey. The day we found out that our health insurance wouldn't cover ANY of my exorbitant medical bills.

My firstborn and his bride – 2022

Jay and I handled this deflating news differently. He was sick with worry and frustration. I sobbed all day with a crushed heart. This was my doing. I shouldn't have driven. I received some hard news the day of the accident and was in no frame of mind to drive that day. And yet, when my daughter asked me to bring extra chairs over for Thanksgiving, I made the choice to drive; a decision that affected myself and others. And now, how will these medical bills effect Jay's retirement? Will he have to work into his 70's just for us to be able to recover from this?"

Secure at Last

My soon-to-be daughter-in-law, sat on the edge of the couch cuddled up next to me as I cried on and off all day. When I told her that I wished I had died, she softly rubbed my leg, and gently told me how much she loved me and how horrible that would have been for our family.

I am so grateful that I never had a time when I felt alone those first two months. Between my family and friends and God, there was so much love poured out, that it comforted me to my very core. And when I found out how many friends on Facebook were praying for my recovery, it warmed and encouraged my heart.

***An analogy: I can be a beautiful Ferrari sitting behind a tow truck. I can be amazingly beautiful to look at, however not working and lacking power. Did I have everything in working order before the accident so that God could use me? No compromise? Any part of my Ferrari that's not in working order thwarts God's use for me. It doesn't matter how I look on the outside to others if I'm not in working order.

I have loved Jesus and His work most of my life. But I've also allowed compromises and distractions to creep in at times. Now these things are glaring; very painful and humbling, yet freeing and necessary, if I am going to be used at my fullest capacity. I want those compromises gone. I want my life to be completely transparent through and through. No hidden compromises. I want to be one with God, with no hidden secrets. No double mindedness.

"Father, I want to be totally transparent, the same inside as I am on the outside. What do you want me to do with the remainder of my life here on earth, Father? That's all that matters to me. That's the only reason I'm back here on this earth and not with You in heaven right now. You miraculously saved me from dying in the accident. Did you send an angel's hand to shield me as I flew through the sunroof? All I know is that if You want me here that much, it must mean that You have a purpose for me here. Make my life strong, powerful, discerning,

Melissa and her family

and miracle-working like You are. Forgive my pride. My weaknesses have been exposed. Let me only boast of Your strength. I give up my selfish goals. I surrender to be a vessel for You to use in any way You desire."

*** *"Mimi!" the kids screamed as all seven came running to my wheelchair. What a different Christmas this was. Melissa did such a good job of getting her house ready for all of us; the job I've always enjoyed doing. Maybe this setback of mine has been good for the next generation to start taking on these responsibilities. And yet, there's a sense of loss even though I'm grateful. So many mixed emotions.*

I was weepy off and on while we were there. The joy of seeing how much love my family has made me realize the sense of loss they would have felt if I had died. Why is it that we don't appreciate each other as much until a near-death experience?

I sat back and listened a lot today. Didn't have my normal desire to be a part of the conversations that were going on. It was kind of nice. At one point, it got a little too loud, so I wheeled myself out of the room. What a strange reaction. I usually thrive on these loud boisterous times. The accident has definitely changed that — at least for now.

199

Secure at Last

***Jay and I had a pretty rough fight yesterday. It went something like this: "I thought we had agreed to curtail our spending." Jay wasn't happy as he came in and found me unwrapping the purchase. "It is totally unnecessary, and I can't believe you ordered this after we talked about the effects of the accident on our finances," he continued. It's a rare occasion that Jay raises his voice like this. My body tensed up like a little girl knowing she's in trouble. "I don't think you respect all that I'm doing trying to juggle everything. I'm the one talking to the doctors and picking up all your prescriptions. I'm the one talking to the police and ambulance company about what happened." No sooner had he finished his raging, and he was out the front door and down the street in his truck.*

I sat in my wheelchair full of my own anger and intense self-loathing. I caused all of this! Normally, I would be right on his heels, getting in my car and going somewhere, anywhere, to escape the tension. But there I sat, trapped in a wheelchair with legs useless to carry me out of this place.

"God, why did this have to happen to me? My life is ruined, my marriage, our finances, our future. I hurt so bad, and I'm scared about our future. How are Jay and I going to get through this? I've wrecked our amazing marriage. How are we going to survive this? I don't want to go through this. Please, God, help me."

When I was done venting, I simply sat there with a downcast head, heart, and soul. I was at the end of myself, which was exactly where I needed to be. God gently whispered, "This could make or break your marriage, Sherry. You will need to bind together and bring every situation, big and small, to Me during this time. If you do, I will build your marriage and make it stronger than it's ever been. If you don't, there will be walls between you that will damage your relationship."

When Jay walked through the front door, I met him in my wheelchair and with tears I shared what God had spoken to my soul. Thank God that Jay is a man of integrity, committed to making our marriage great. He quietly took my hand and asked forgiveness for his anger. I asked forgiveness for being insensitive to our financial situation. We prayed together that God would help us treat one another with the grace that God had so freely given to us. We prayed that God would protect our marriage

My mode of transportation

through this time and make us an even stronger example of a godly marriage. I want this to be the pattern for facing each ordeal up ahead.

***After the accident, I learned that the woman in the other SUV was six months pregnant with her first child. I can't tell you how horrible it felt to know that an innocent mom and baby were affected. My heart was scared and crushed for her and her baby. Jay and I searched for anyone in our community who might know about their condition. We were given some vague answers that she had broken her sternum and a couple of ribs, but we wanted more details. I wept for her and prayed fervently that she and the baby would have no lasting repercussions from the impact. Feeling responsible for the accident, I'm not sure how I would have handled it if her innocent baby were to have suffered or been harmed in any way.

I remembered back to when I was pregnant with Nathan. I took every precaution to make sure my baby and I were healthy. This mama must have felt a dreadful fear that her child could potentially suffer some trauma from the impact of the accident.

"God, I think about the lady in the other car. How hurt was she? How scared was she for her baby? How much pain and suffering did she have to go through? Is she angry with me? God if there is a way to bring forgiveness and healing between us, that would be such an amazing thing. Please God, heal her emotions

201

whatever they are on this. You know way more than I do, so meet her, Father, and heal any pain she may have. Thank You, that You love her immensely and want to heal her even more than I do. I pray Your will be done in her life.

"Sherry, I just found out that a miracle happened before the impact that just might have saved the woman's baby from more harm," a mutual friend excitedly told me. "Apparently, just before your cars collided, the mama loosened her seat belt to go down under her belly. Apparently, she had needed to use the bathroom, and the belt was pressing down uncomfortably on her bladder." This was absolutely fabulous news to my ears.

"Father, thank you so much for being the great protector," I poured out my heart full of gratitude and relief. "You covered that baby with Your hand and kept him safe in the car, and I am forever grateful, Lord. Please continue to form every detail of the baby's body perfectly as he continues to grow inside the womb. And be with his mama to give her peace and trust as she continues carrying the baby inside her body."

A few months later came this welcomed news: "Hey, Sherry, did you hear that the lady in the car accident had her baby?" My friend, who knew how anxious I was over the baby's health, had come right over to share the news with me.

"Really? Tell me, oh, my gosh, tell me, is he Ok? Is he healthy?" I was both nervous and excited at the same time.

"He was born a perfectly healthy baby boy. Mommy and baby are doing good!"

I let out an audible scream as my hands flew up in the air, "Yaaaaay!!! Oh my gosh, that's the best news ever. Thank you, Jesus!" That night I slept a little sounder knowing that all was well with this precious little one.

Two months into recovery, I was walking to the bathroom when my leg buckled, and I fell to the floor with crippling pain. "AHHHH! What on earth is that?" I screamed while trying to get up. No matter how I maneuvered my legs, they just wouldn't support my weight. After a few minutes on the floor, I used my arms to pull myself up to a sitting position. *Oh God, don't let me have a setback. It's already been 8 weeks. I just want to get better. Pleeeeease help me, Lord.*

After resting for a few minutes, I belly-crawled over to the bed. I sat there for a while not sure of how to get back to the front of the house. Doubts and fears spun in my head, with frustration and defeat following right behind. I tried several ways to stand and walk, each time falling back onto the bed in pain. After a few minutes, I discovered that if I used only the good leg, I could shimmy my foot left to right and then right to left. Slowly I got down the hallway and finally into the living room. I sat on the couch in a pile of sweat. *Lord, no! I don't want to go through any more setbacks.*

It took a few weeks to be seen by a doctor. As I sat in the waiting room, I wondered, *Will I ever be able to hike the rocks down to our neighborhood river with the grandkids? Will I be able to race, jump on the trampoline, or play ball with them like I used to?* My thoughts were interrupted, "Ms. Francis?"

"Right here," I replied, as Jay helped me with my walker. I had tried to get this appointment with a specialist three times, and each time they said they wouldn't see me because it wasn't their field. Frustrating!

When Dr. Lee walked into the room, he had a resolved look on his face. "Ms. Francis, I have looked at your CT scan and X-ray results. You have a torn quad muscle with two hematomas on each side. Can I take a look at your leg? Here, just lie down here, and let me see how far your range is." After manipulating and putting pressure on my leg in several directions, he said, "Well, it looks like you have pretty good range of motion for what you've been through. Go ahead and stand up.

When I stood up, he felt the dip in my left leg, my good leg. With a surprised look on his face he said, "Yeah, that is a pretty significant tear in your quad. You're definitely going to have muscle strength loss."

"But Doctor," I said with expectancy, "I've heard that the muscle can be sown back together?"

A look of amusement came over his face. "Let me put it this way. Can you sew up hamburger meat?"

I didn't see anything comical about this. "Well, no." I replied, knowing where he was going with this.

"Ms. Francis, your quad muscle was pulverized. There's no way of sewing what's left of your muscle back together again because it's the consistency of hamburger."

"Ok!" I swallowed hard. "How will this affect the use of my leg in the future?"

"Well, you'll probably lose about 20% of the strength in that leg. I doubt you'll be jumping up and down or doing any kind of jarring aerobics anyway, right? I mean you're 61. You know, if you do aerobics, you'll want to do low impact, not jarring the leg. You must look at it this way: you could be dead or without the use of your legs at all. At least you are walking right?"

Initially I wanted to say, *Yeah, maybe you would you care a little more if it was your leg. You have no idea how active I am as a 61-year-old woman.* But I abstained.

At home, I brought this new challenge to the Lord, and again He gave me His peace and assurance that if I remained in His will, He would take care of me.

"I'm really not worried," I found myself saying to Geri, my physical therapist. "I'm honestly not afraid of the outcome. And I think it's because I am being taught that God is in control of everything in my life. I can trust Him completely for whatever comes my way, knowing that the One Who loves me perfectly is trustworthy. Because He lives in me, I have His peace and joy through anything I face. I think I'm finally understanding a little of how Paul and Silas could be singing and rejoicing in shackles right after being beaten. It's GOD'S PRESENCE!"

This would not have been my automatic response in the past. I'm very competitive and love to be fully engaged in sports and activities. However, when talking with a friend about this, I realized that being sedentary hadn't been as devastatingly hard as I expected. The nearness of God's presence had replaced the need in my life to be busy with activities. Although I had been stuck in this wounded, limited body, I was experiencing more fulfillment and joy than I had ever known. Wow!

I now realize that so much of my life, I had chased after good times: vacations, BBQ get togethers, parties, sports activities, and other activities, to fill the empty places in my heart. Now, with all those other things stripped away due to my broken body, I was experiencing more joy than those activities had ever provided. How did that happen? It took an accident to slow me down, so that I could seek God and rely only on Him, with my whole heart. I could see that the part of me that needed fun and excitement to achieve happiness, had now been wholly and completely fulfilled and satisfied by God's presence. Talking to Him throughout the day and enjoying His rich, loving presence was now fulfilling the longing in my heart for more out of life. And nobody, or nothing, could take this away.

In the third month, the swelling from the rod and screws in my leg started to come down. Jay and I were shocked to find that the screws holding my broken right kneecap together were literally coming out the other side. If anything happened to touch that area, it was like a hot, searing knife penetrating my knee. We figured something had to be wrong, so after another hospital visit and Xray, it was apparent the screws were too long for the size of my knee. The surgeon didn't admit to any wrongdoing. Only an explanation that the robot machine that was used must have miscalculated the

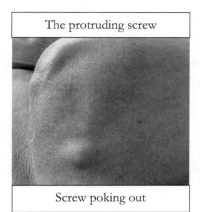

The protruding screw

Screw poking out

length of screws. It was the robot's fault. Hence, another surgery to replace the screws. And another huge invoice to add to our pile of medical bills.

As I said earlier, my medical bills were exorbitant, and we weren't sure how we were going to pay for it all. Jay had talked to Kaiser's medical billing several times to see if there was any way to negotiate the price and had been shut down each time. We were somewhat discouraged but realized that God would give us grace to walk through whatever the outcome.

On yet another phone call to the billing department, Jay was asking another person if there was any way of negotiating the amount. Surprisingly, for the first time the lady mentioned an organization that helped subsidize large medical bills. She said that she would reach out to the department and see if they would take on our case. Jay filled out all the necessary paperwork that included our income, and the lady said she would contact him with their answer. When we didn't hear anything back for weeks, we somewhat resigned in our hearts that our case had been turned down. Our income was nowhere near poverty, so we figured we didn't qualify.

We really didn't want to hear this bad news, so we didn't contact the billing company for quite a while. We figured: *no* news wasn't as bad as *bad* news. Finally, we decided to face the verdict, and Jay made the call. At first the lady said that we still needed to pay the entire bill. Jay reminded her that we had applied for help, after which she scrolled down the computer screen to the bottom.

"Oh, wait sir, there's something on the bottom that says…hmmm it says zero balance. Yeah, looks like you don't owe any money," she replied without emotion.

Jay couldn't believe what he was hearing. He hung up the phone in silence, and just sat there, trying to take in the enormity of that statement. When he shared the news with me, we both just stared at each other with eyes and mouths wide open. It was almost as if we didn't want to get too excited in case it wasn't true. We decided that we would believe it when we read it on our statement. How's that for faith?

Every month when the statement was posted, we would take a peek to see if our balance had changed to zero. Nothing changed for three months. We started to doubt what the lady had told us. During these months, it was if God was saying *Just trust in My will for you.*

Sure enough, after three months we opened our statement and the balance staring us in the face was ZERO! Again, Jay and I were so incredibly humbled that God would have such mercy to create another miracle for us. *How could it be? I created this mess. God, Your goodness is so undeserved.* We continue to feel His love and thank Him from the bottom of our hearts every time we think of this miracle.

During the process of healing, I have been sure of this one thing; that God supernaturally protected my flight through the sunroof and saved me from death for a purpose. About three months after the accident, I decided to ask Him what that purpose was. He quietly spoke in my heart that He wanted me to write a book on the story of my life.

"God," I queried, "nobody's going to be interested in my life. There's so much going on with the Covid Virus and the world right now. Why would anybody be interested in a no-name like me? But, Lord, I'll tell you what, if You have someone tomorrow tell me that I should write a book about my life, I will know it's Your voice and obey You."

The next day was the first day that I was starting back to teach piano lessons again since the accident. I answered the door in my wheelchair for student Seraphina and her mom Joni. As per her usual sunny personality, Joni bubbled, "Sherry, you look so much better than I imagined. With all you've been through, have you ever thought of writing a book? I mean you've had so many setbacks in your life and have come through them without being bitter. I know that Jesus is important in your life, so maybe you should write about it."

teaching Ella

Back to my passion – teaching piano

I threw my head up in the air and laughingly responded, "Oh my gosh, Joni, you're never going to believe this, but I just asked God to give me a sign today if He wants me to write a book."

"Well, there you go. You better start writing," she laughed.

A Christian with pure faith would have taken this as a definite sign from heaven. But not me. No, I needed one more sign. Writing a book takes a tremendous amount of time and I wanted to be sure this was really what God wanted. "Ok, if this is really You God, make this happen again tomorrow. If one more person tomorrow mentions a book, I'll really know it's You."

Sure enough, the next day I opened an email and read my Aunt Bev's words: "Sherry, if you ever want to write a book, here are some questions you should answer. Send them back to me and we'll discuss it." My Aunt is a published author and has taught writing seminars to hundreds of people around the world. That pretty much sealed the deal for me. I knew that I had heard from God, and He wanted me to write. I knew instantly what my takeaway from the book would be, *how to go from victim to overcomer; how to overcome life's tragedies.*

So, I started writing a few months ago with you, the reader in mind. Both your daily journey and mine include joys as well as sorrows. How do we react to the tragedies of life? While writing my story, I have been ruthlessly honest, exposing some things about me that I wasn't sure I wanted anybody to know. I've done it all for you because I know you've experience tragedies that you didn't cause as well as some that you have caused. Jesus takes us in whatever circumstance we find ourselves and loves us completely. His desire is for us to heal and be restored. But it takes work and surrender. I hope through these pages you have found some tools to help you stand up and overcome.

Every one of us is a potential diamond in the rough. Embedded within each person are diamond-like qualities waiting to be mined. Are we willing to endure the pressure, the cutting, and the polishing of the Master Jeweler to bring out the diamond inside us? Most of us are not. But, for those of you who really want your diamond to break out in magnificent radiance and stunning beauty, take note.

From all I've gone through, I am telling you, "It's worth it." Would I have chosen this crazy bumpy life? Not in a million years. Yet I know that I wouldn't know Jesus the way I do. I wouldn't be *Secure at Last* in God's perfect love and acceptance that helps me love myself. Nor would I know His settled peace that goes beyond my understanding through any situation. I wouldn't have patience and kindness, compassion, and empathy that springs from being able to relate to others in trouble. If I have any wisdom to share with others, it's because of the extreme pressure, cutting and polishing done on my inner stone. I would be much more self-absorbed, instead of having an enormous love for God and others.

My prayer for you is that whatever messy situation you may find yourself in, you will decide that you don't want to be the victim anymore. It seems that the world right now loves to celebrate victims. Yet if you stay the victim, you will remain in your misery and live life far beneath the potential God created for you. Or you can live a fulfilling life that is free of anger, fear and perpetual sadness. I am here as evidence of that. There is a better way! And it all starts with a choice. Your choice. Nobody else can make it for you. What will you choose? I implore you to choose the life of an overcomer.

As I write this now, God has done another miracle in my life. This one I wasn't even asking for. I know this body is temporary and short lived. The pain I experienced daily continued to be a reminder of the imperfection that we have here on earth. And since it's so temporary I had stopped asking for physical healing. My friends and family had not.

At 5:00 AM on July 26th, exactly eight months after the accident, a loud voice in my head woke me up. "Rise and be healed in the name of Jesus!"

What was that? I thought, as I rubbed my sleepy eyes. The voice continued to resonate in my ears as I tried to figure out if this was God's voice or my own. Jay was already up and working in the office. *Ok let's find out if this is God's voice,* I thought out loud. I pulled the covers back and hoisted my legs over the bed and to the floor. Slowly I started walking around my room. Heel, toe, heel, toe. I knew something was different! My usual limp-along gait was straight. My hip wasn't out of place as it had been. I stopped walking and stood straight and looked down at my feet. They were both equally touching the floor, where before my injured leg had been shorter.

As I walked around my bedroom, the tears streamed. It had definitely been God's voice healing me! I walked into Jay's office and told him what had just happened. Another amazing undeserved miracle. How great God's love is! As I write this, I have been walking without a limp for eight months now. Even my doctor has admitted this was nothing short of a miracle.

Of all the miracles God did throughout my recovery, the one I cherish the most is the nearness of His presence! Nobody can take away the joy, peace, and true satisfaction that walking through life in His presence brings. Sure, life may bring some more bumps and bruises, but with His tools around my belt and His presence, I plan to be an overcomer! I am *Secure at Last!*

Jay and me on a recent trip – God is so awesome!

About the Author

Sherry Francis is an accomplished musician, has sung and played in many countries, started three Schools of Music, accompanied well-known vocalists on stage and on air. She was a pastor's wife and foreign missionary in various islands in the Pacific.

Today she is semiretired. She provides private piano lessons to adults and children, plays piano for her home church, and mentors and counsels women.

Sherry has two adult children and nine grandchildren. She lives in Northern California.

She would love to hear from you, especially if this story has been a help or encouragement to you: sherry1712@yahoo.com

Printed in Great Britain
by Amazon

33287198R00123